Never Fry Bacon in the Nude
and other life lessons

O. Gene Bicknell

Never Fry Bacon in the Nude
By O. Gene Bicknell
Copyright © 2002 by Williams Publishing
All rights reserved. Printed in the United States of America. No part of this book may be reproduced or transmitted in any form or by any means, electronic or mechanical, including photocopying, recording, or by any information storage and retrieval system without written permission from Williams Publishing, except for the inclusions of quotations in a review.

Publisher's Note

This publication is designed to provide accurate and authoritative information in regard to the subject matter covered. It is sold with the understanding that the publisher is not engaged in rendering psychological, financial, legal or other professional services. If expert assistance or counseling is needed, the services of a competent professional should be sought.

For information contact: Williams Publishing, 203 E. Laverne Way, Palm Springs, California 92264, Telephone: (760) 318-3407.

Cover Design by Draco Digital.
Text Design by Arte Moderno.

Distributed in U.S.A. by Williams Publishing

Library of Congress Catalog Card Number: 2001092952
ISBN 0-9666906-1-3

Publisher's Cataloging-in-Publication
(Provided by Quality Books, Inc.)

Bicknell, O. Gene.
Never fry Bacon in the nude! : and othe life lessons
/ O.Gene Bicknell. -- 1st ed.
p. cm.
LCCN 2001092952
ISBN 0-9666906-1-3

1. Motivation (Psychology) 2. Entrepreneurship
3. Self-actualization (Psychology) 4. Self-help
techniques. I. Title.

BF503.B53 2002 158.1
QBI01-700863

Acknowledgements

Any birthing, be it baby or book, is strenuous and seldom done alone. Many people have contributed to this book simply by intersecting my life and efforts to find and achieve my personal success. Most of you know who you are and that you have my gratitude and appreciation.

However, two people were especially instrumental in the preparation of this material. Cindy Allen, thank you for some of the original editing, support and suggestions during the early stages of finalizing the material. Cindy helped immensely with the structure and organization of my notes.

Joycie King, editor author and friend. Her editing, sentence structuring, phrasing, verbiage and organization were the crowning support for finishing this book. Joycie's background and experience were invaluable in finalizing and reviewing our reworks. Her efforts, belief in the material and commitment were very heartfelt and most appreciated.

I also wish to thank Karen Badart, Cindy Morris, Dr. Bill Rose and all my friends and associates who have helped me with the completion of this book project.

And last but not least, a special note of appreciation to my lovely wife Rita, for all of her support and belief in me and this book.

Preface

<u>Never Fry Bacon in the Nude</u> is an analogy I've used many times when talking about the vulnerabilities of business. If you're not prepared and in the proper frame of mind (properly clothed), you run the risk of taking some pretty heavy-duty burns in some not-so-nice places.

The purpose of this book is to share the many philosophies that I have encountered over the years. Most of the material is certainly not original, as any material is not truly original. I don't expect this book to change anyone's life. No one can change another person. We can only change ourselves, and to do this we must first want to change.

This is a book about developing yourself, not only personally but professionally. Many times we forget that these two entities are very closely intertwined. Most of the material is theories and practices I have found useful in the business world. The anec-dotes have come from friends, acquaintances and business associates-from the many different people I have had contact with through my years in business. They are ideas that have worked for me and worked for others. These ideas range from a concept we call "termite control," to the art of listening. There is also information regarding the business plan, since this is the foundation from which to build a successful business.

The intent of this book is to make the reader think about how he or she can apply these ideas to their own situations and business projects. You probably know these things, may have even used them, and though they worked well, for some reason you have stopped. I do hope the theories, suggestions and anecdotes provided will stimulate your desire to change and help you become the successful person you want to be.

Glean from it what you may, as I have gleaned from my lifetime of experiences and associations. This is the kind of book where YOU write the ending. After all, YOU are the ultimate end!

INTRODUCTION

You Learn As You Go

At the age of eleven I went to work in a bakery. I received ten cents an hour for 40 hours a week. At least I was paid for 40 hours. I actually worked 70 - 80 hours. People valued a job more in those times. There were no resources for complaints. Most people were glad to have a job, so I worked my 70 hours, was paid for 40 and appreciated my good fortune.

The wife of the baker hired me. There was a small cafe on one side, with a counter and stools. The bakery was on the other side. I worked in the back room with the baker. It didn't take me long to figure out that the person who would have the most influence on me in that shop was the baker's wife.

Her personality influenced everything and everyone in that bakery, customer and worker alike. She was one of the most cantankerous, negative people I have ever met! Her abrasive personality lost a good many customers, including my sister. Ada came in one day for some bakery items. As the baker's wife crossed over to the cafe to get some change my sister decided to follow her. She was trying to save the woman a trip back across the shop.

"Get back over there," the woman screeched at Ada. "I'll bring it back to you!"

My poor sister was so shaken she left the store never to return. Unfortunately, she was not the only customer to feel the impact of this woman's personality. Things like this happened almost daily. From my position in the back room, even at eleven, I was puzzled by the woman's behavior. She depended on her customers for her living and yet she was belligerent, abusive and dealt with them in a negative manner. To me, it was a perfect example of how NOT to treat customers. In spite of her attitude and behavior, I got along well with her. The example she set challenged me to learn how to get along with people. I also learned how to work hard and not expect much gratitude in return.

Apparently I had some effect on her as well. We stayed in contact and after the death of her husband, she looked upon me as family. Because of her unpleasant disposition, none of her relatives maintained any contact or communication with her. In her elder years it was necessary for her to be in a nursing home and, at her request, I became her custodian. I provided for her care, paid her bills and in the end was responsible for most of her burial expenses. We never know what impact someone will have on our lives.

By the time I was twelve I had progressed up the career ladder to a job as a soda jerk. I wasn't very big for my age and had a hard time reaching over the counter. But, I worked hard and dedicated myself to becoming the best soda jerk I could be. I was successful, too, as I held that job for nearly three years.

This experience provided yet another important lesson in dealing with people. Two brothers owned the drugstore—one a big, jolly type and easy to get along with; the other, smaller brother was more difficult. The pharmacists took turns on shifts, and their contrasting personalities taught me a great deal about the importance of being flexible when dealing with people.

I moved from soda jerk to a sacker in a grocery store. Ted, the man I worked for at the grocery store was the hardest driving person I have ever known. The people who worked in that store never stopped working! If we weren't serving customers or carrying out huge sacks of groceries to their cars, we were busy stocking shelves. If he caught anyone sitting down or resting while on the job, we all heard about it—believe me, the message came across loud and clear! From his example I learned about the "dictatorial style" of management. It worked for him. In his defense, I must say that he was a conservative but good investor. These traits made him a successful business man. I learned a lot from Ted and admired him. Hard work was a non-negotiable requirement with him.

My next experience was as a fry cook and from there I went to work in a butcher's shop. All along the way, I listened, observed and learned valuable lessons from my employers. Some were about how to treat people, run a business and be success-ful. Some were about how NOT to do those things.

As a youngster I was extremely intimidated by anyone with power and wealth. I came from a poor family, and it was impor-tant for me to work hard and keep those jobs. My life and my contribution to my family depended on what I earned. This made my bosses seem even more powerful and intimidating.

From the time I started at the bakery, I bought my own clothes, earned my own spending money, provided my own transportation and paid my own school expenses. My parents provided my meals and a place to sleep. And, they both were both working harder than I was just to provide our home.

As I look back, I realize I learned more through example than by verbal instructions. No one said "do this" or "do that" and you'll be a success. Rather, I watched and observed what worked and what didn't. From these experiences I developed three essential values to which I attribute my later success....work hard, be honest and be flexible in dealing with other people. I learned by observing my parents, my employers and the people with whom they interacted. While different busi-nesses require different outlooks and techniques, these three things never change. They are the essence of every successful business relationship.

Contents

Acknowledgments

Preface

Introduction

Part 1 - Characteristics of Success
Hard Work
Little Engine That Could
Most Valuable Asset
Nothing Stays The Same

Part 2 - Looking Within
Make Yourself Better
Self Analysis
The Art of Communication
Wanted...A Good Listener
What You Don't Know CAN Hurt You
Ego...Beware of Empire Building

Part 3 - Developing Our Skills
Exploring Ambitions
Improving Our Abilities
Make Your First Impression A Good One
Inherent Versus Learned
Have A Little Compassion

Part 4 - Leadership Creates Success
Motivating Our People To Want To Succeed
Characteristics of Leadership
No "I" in Team
Living With The Reality of Change
Tolerance - A Necessity

Part 5 - A Business of Your Own
The Making of An Entrepreneur
Picture Your Business
Conservatism Is The Key
Like It Or Not, Government Affects Your Business
Emotion, The New Economic Indicator
The Reality of Investment
Opportunities Abound in the International Community
The Economic and Global Picture of Today's Marketplace and
Forecasting for Conditions Into The Next Century

PART I

CHARACTERISTICS OF SUCCESS

1
All It Takes Is A Little Hard Work

The $5 Job

No one in our small Utah town knew where the Countess had come from. Her careful, precise English indicated that she was not from America. From the size of her house and staff, we knew that she must be wealthy. She never entertained, and she made it clear that when she was at home, she was inaccessible. Only when she stepped outdoors did she become a public figure. To a small fry, like me, she was held in awe.

The Countess always carried a cane, not only for support, but as a means of chastising youngsters who she thought needed disciplining. At one time or another, most of the youngsters in our neighborhood seemed to display that need. By running fast and staying alert, I managed to stay out of her reach. But one day, when I was about thirteen, I was short-cutting through her hedge and she got close enough to rap my head with her stick.

"Young man," she said. "I want to talk to you."

I was expecting a lecture on the evils of trespassing, but as she looked at me, half smiling, she seemed to have changed her mind.

"Don't you live in that green house with the yellow trim, over in the next block?" she asked.

"Yes ma'am."

"Do you take care of your lawn, water it, clip it, mow it?"

"Yes."

"Good, I've lost my gardener. Be at my house Thursday morning at 7 a.m., and don't tell me you have something else to do," she commanded. "I've seen you slouching on Thursdays."

When the Countess gave an order, it was carried out. I didn't dare not go on Thursday.

I clipped her whole lawn three times before she was satisfied. And even then, she had me down on all fours, looking for weeds, until my knees were as green as the grass. She finally called me up on the porch and asked, "Well, young man, how much do you want for your day's work?"

"I don't know, 50 cents maybe," I replied.

"Is that what you think you're worth?"

"Yes ma'am, about that."

"Very well," she said. "Here's the 50 cents you say you're worth, and here's the dollar-fifty I earned for you by pushing you. Now, I'm going to tell you something about how you and I are going to work together. There are as many ways to mow a lawn as there are people. And, they may be worth anywhere from a penny to $5. Let's say that a $3 job would be about what you have done today, except that you would do it all by yourself. A $4 job would be something so perfect that you'd have to be something of a fool to spend that much time on a lawn. A $5 job is, well, impossible, so we'll forget about that. Now then, each week I'm going to pay you according to your own evaluation of your work," she said.

I left with my $2, richer than I remember being in my whole life. I determined I was going to get $4 out of her next time.

But, I failed to reach even the $3 mark. My will began to falter the second time around her yard.

"$2 again, huh?" I asked.

"That kind of job puts you right on the edge of being dismissed, young man," she said.

"Yes ma'am, I'll do better next week," I promised. And somehow I did. The last time around the yard, I was exhausted, but I found I could spur myself on. In the exhilaration of that new feeling I had no hesitation in asking the Countess for $3.

Each Thursday for the next few weeks, I became more acquainted with her lawn. Places where the ground was a little high or low. Places that needed to be clipped short or left long on the edges to make a more satisfying curve along the garden. Then I became more aware of what would be considered a $4 job. And each week I would resolve to do just that kind of job.

By the time I had made the $3 or $3.50 mark, I was too exhausted to remember even having the ambition to go beyond that point.

"You look like a good, consistent $3 man," she replied as she handed me the money. "Well, don't feel too bad," she would try to comfort me. "After all, there are only a handful of people in the world who could do a $4 job."

Her words were comforting to me at first, but then they became an irritant. It made me resolve to do a $4 job, even if killed me. In the fever of my resolve, I could see myself expiring on her lawn, with the Countess leaning over me, handing me $4 with a tear in her eye, begging my forgiveness for having thought I could not do it.

It was in the middle of such a fever on a Thursday night when I was trying to forget the day's defeat and get some *sleep, that the truth really hit me. It hit me so hard I sat upright, half choking on my excitement. It was the $5 job I had to do; not the $4 job! I had to do the job that no one else could do, because it was impossible.*

I was well acquainted with the difficulties ahead. I had the problem, for example, of doing something about the worm mounds on the lawn. The Countess might not have even noticed them they were so small, but in my bare feet, I knew about them. I could go on trimming the garden edges with shears, but I knew that a $5 job demanded that I line up each edge with a yard stick and then trim it precisely with an edger.

I started the next Thursday by ironing out the worm mounds with a heavy roller. After two hours of that, I was ready to give up for the day. It was 9:00 in the morning and my will was already gone. It was only by accident that I regained it. Sitting under a walnut tree for a few moments, after finishing the rolling, I surveyed the job. The lawn looked so good and felt so good under my feet, I was anxious to get on with it. I followed this renewal secret for the rest of the day. I stopped for a few minutes every hour, reviewing, so I could regain my perspective.

Between reviews I mowed four times. Two times length wise and two times across, until the yard looked like a velvet checkerboard. Then I dug around every tree, crumbling the big clods and smoothing the soil with my hands; then finished with the edger, meticulously lining up each stroke so the effect would be perfectly symmetrical. I carefully trimmed the grass between the flagstones and the front walk. The shears wore my fingers raw, but the walk had never looked better.

Finally, about 8:00 that evening, it was all completed. I was so proud, I didn't even feel tired when I went to the door.

"Well, what is it today?", the Countess asked.

"$5", I said, trying for a little calm and sophistication.

"$5? You mean $4 don't you? I told you that a $5 was impossible."

"No, it isn't," I said. "I just did it."

"Well, young man," she exclaimed. "The first $5 job in history deserves some looking around."

We walked about the lawn together in the light of the evening, and even I was overcome by the possibility of what I had done.

"Young man," she said, putting her hand on my shoulder. "What on earth made you do such a crazy, wonderful thing?"

I didn't know why. Even if I did, I couldn't have explained it.

She continued, "I think I know how you felt when this idea first came into your head. The idea of caring for a lawn that I told you was impossible to accomplish. It made you very happy when it first came to you, then a little frightened, am I right?"

She could see by the startled look on my face that she was.

"I know how you felt, because the same thing happens to almost everyone," she said. "They feel this sudden burst in them, of wanting to do something great. They feel this wonderful happiness, but then it passes because they've talked themselves out of it because it's impossible."

Although I don't know the author of this story, it spoke to me when I first read it. I think it speaks volumes about where motivation comes from. Whenever something in you says it's impossible, remember to take a careful look to see if it isn't God, asking you to grow an inch, a foot or a mile so that you may come to a fuller life.

You have the capability of doing a $5 job, but there are no guarantees. You can win, or you can lose. There's an opportunity to excel or to be great, and it comes in many forms, shapes and sizes. But it's all up to you!

There are No Get Rich Schemes.
There are Only Good Ideas,
a Conservative Approach and Hard Work.

Dreamers

Throughout your lifetime, people will come to you with get-rich-quick schemes. They will attempt to lure you into an investment that they claim to be a guaranteed success, with no effort on your part—easy money. They may have a stock tip or insider information on a company that is going to do well.

Back in the days of the oil boom, I used to get about five calls a week from people who wanted to cut me in on some "sweet deal."

"...There's an oil well right next to where we're drilling and it's producing a thousand barrels a day," they'd say.

"Don't you have any relatives, any friends?" I'd ask.

"Well, yeah."

"And have you ever met me?"

To their "no," I would respond, "Then why in the world would you want to give me this "sweet deal" when you have friends and relatives that could benefit from it?"

There are several kinds of dreamers - one is a promoter who believes in the get-rich-schemes because he wants to believe in an easy way to fortune and success. There are people who want to talk their way into prosperity. They'll say they want to be millionaires, but they don't want to work to make it a reality.

Then, there is the other kind of dreamer. This person has a vision - a desire - a goal he wants to achieve. But this person isn't going to just talk about it or try to get others to make his dream happen. He is willing to put in the time, the effort, the hard work, whatever money he's got and the sacrifice to make his dream become a reality. He doesn't look to someone else to do the work for him or to invest all the money in his idea.

This dreamer has a good idea or a career goal in mind. He develops a plan to get to that goal. He's optimistic and positive-minded. He BELIEVES in himself and in his dream. He's ready to set out and make that dream become a REALITY. But too often the plan falls by the wayside if he doesn't stick to his plan and isn't willing to pay the price. Dreams only come true when the magic of commitment plays out all the effort into completion.

Achievers

There are lots of dreamers out there. As the first example shows, not all dreamers are achievers. An achiever has a dream and a vision. He sets realistic goals and steps to become a success. This doesn't mean he only sets goals he KNOWS he can reach. An achiever sets goals that are high, but not completely out of reach. She knows she's taking a chance at failure, but it doesn't deter her.

The ultimate in achievement comes from desire and determination. The ability to excel comes from within. The sprinter wins the race in the last 20 yards. When others fall back, she reaches deep down inside and pulls that little bit of extra adrenaline to make the difference. The achiever is a doer.

The quest for knowledge and personal improvement is a daily ritual among the doers. The winners never bet on a race unless they're in it. They don't depend on someone else to win for them; they want to be involved with the way the race is run.

The opportunity to leave a legacy, long remembered after we are gone, is seldom available to most of us. There are only a few individuals who can accomplish that. Those people are either extremely talented, very lucky or they contribute long hours of tireless effort to a task or mission in an effort to achieve a purpose or contribute to a noteworthy cause.

Be a Doer, Not a Talker

We often establish a high goal for ourselves. We convince ourselves that we can do a particular thing and we set out to accomplish our objective. Sometimes we feel it is important to let everyone know about our ambition.

Now the reality! There are times when our mouth overloads our brain and we find ourselves square in the middle of an undertaking that is not as easy as we thought it would be. Many times we speak too quickly. Then, for some reason-time constraints, family or outside responsibilities-something inter-feres with our freedom to complete or conduct the activity nec-essary to do what we have told everyone we are going to do.

We also might find, with time, that we don't want the mis-sion as much as we first did. Our motivation and commitment wanes. This leaves us with the embarrassment of "eating crow" or having to make excuses for why we can't do what we said we were going to do.

If you have an id... to do is resist the urge ... encouraging yourself, but achieve your objective ...., talk about it.

*They who tread through thick and thin
And keep their spirit to do it again,
Will not have to try to impress their friends
Because their friends will do it for them.
But if we only talk and talk,
But are yet unwilling to walk the walk,
The air that leaks between our lips
Will not be heard as viable tips,
But only a waste of valuable time
For what they want is only in their mind.*

OGB

Stamina or Stick To-Itiveness

"If you ain't lazy and you ain't afraid, you can do a lot."

A true achiever knows there may be difficulties along the way, but he won't quit. A true achiever certainly isn't lazy. He resists the temptation to give in to the exhaustion of hard work and commitment to accomplish his dream. A great athlete, who is so tired that it would be easy to quit or give up, instead must tap that inner resource down deep inside and pull from that determination that says, "I want to be a winner." It's easier to quit, but the emptiness it causes never quite leaves because you know you didn't give your all and you weren't willing to pay the price.

Be your own self-prophecy! Say you will and then "do it!"

The poet, Edgar B. Guest, defined hard work and stamina as follows:

It Couldn't Be Done

Somebody said that it couldn't be done,
But he with a chuckle replied
That "maybe it couldn't," but he would be one
Who wouldn't say so 'til he'd tried.
So he buckled right in with the trace of a grin
On his face. If he worried he hid it.
He started to sing as he tackled the thing
That couldn't be done, and he did it.

Somebody scoffed: "Oh, you'll never do that;
At least no one ever has done it";
But he took off his coat and he took off his hat,
And the first thing we knew he'd begun it.
With a lift of his chin and a bit of a grin,
Without any doubting or quiddit,
He started to sing as he tackled the thing
That couldn't be done, and he did it.

There are thousands to tell you it cannot be done,
There are thousands to prophesy failure;
There are thousands to point out to you one by one,
The dangers that wait to assail you.
But just buckle in with a bit of a grin,
Just take off your coat and go to it;
Just start in to sing as you tackle the thing
That "cannot be done," and you'll do it.

Another old saying that dreamers who are achievers live by is,

"There are no problems, only correction opportunities." When things don't seem to be going our way we can do two things. We can stop trying and give up, or we can give it our best shot and keep going. We can look for the possible "opportunities" to correct our perceived problems.

In many small communities, some retailers viewed the arrival of the big discount houses as a potential problem. It is very difficult for a small retail business to compete with a big discount house. However, many small retailers were challenged to look for ways to be profitable. By being creative, doing research and looking for "opportunities" that the big discount houses can't offer-things like personal service, knowledge of their product, special or custom orders-many of these retailers have been successful and many of our small downtowns are still thriving. The secret is to find a niche and perfect it.

Don't Quit

When things go wrong as they sometimes will
When the road you're trudging seems all uphill,
When funds are low and the debts are high,
And you want to smile, but you have to sigh,
When care is pressing you down a bit
Rest if you must, but don't you quit!
Success is failure turned inside out,
The silver tint of the clouds of doubt,
And you can never tell how close you are,
It may be near when it seems afar.
So, stick to the fight when you're hardest hit,
It's when things go wrong that you mustn't quit!
(Author unknown)

Dreaming Realistically - Set a Timeline

Even with strong effort, dedicated purpose or undying optimism, dreams sometimes don't become reality. It's wonderful to have a dream and the vision to make that dream a reality. However, we also have to know when things just aren't going to work out. We have to be ready to be flexible if our dream begins to unravel.

The entertainment business is a good example. This industry constantly leaves a trail of "hangers-on" who commit most of their lives to being in the business; looking for that one major "break."

Most earn little money and live meagerly because they are unwilling to be flexible. They pitch deals, go to interview after interview and receive rejection after rejection, but still they hang on, living and hoping for their "big break."

Unfortunately, it seldom happens. I understand how it feels. I've been there. I had dreams of being in the entertainment business; of the project or deal that was just ahead, that was sure to materialize tomorrow. But, I realized early on that this happens for only a few; maybe one or two percent. I still enjoy the entertainment field, the contacts and opportunities that sometimes come my way. But, as I said, I found out early that it wasn't going to be my bread and butter. It's still a part of my life, but it's not ALL my life. I've found other ways to be successful and happy.

Being realistic is difficult. In order not to waste precious time on this earth, it's important to have not only a goal, but also a deadline. We must work hard and give it our all, but we also need to set a realistic timeline in which to achieve success in that field or business.

As your life progresses, your desires and needs change. Your ambitions and objectives should, therefore, be well thought out, obtainable, practical and with a <u>timeline for completion</u>.

Strive to be the Best
Mediocrity is Based in Negative Thought.

We all experience extreme peaks and valleys in our lives. Those peaks and valleys transcend to the level that we allow them to transcend.

People who are successful find a way to make those peaks and valleys level out. If you can keep the ridges from becoming too high and the valleys from becoming too low, the less weight you will carry. Try to stay on an even keel and you'll be more successful and productive.

It's a constant battle to keep a positive frame of mind. The challenge is to not get overwrought by these downturns and failures. Handle them as well as you handle the successes. If you don't constantly reinforce a positive attitude, you let yourself get down and the next thing you know depression has immobilized you. The biggest saboteur to any daily plan or working environment is stress levels and negative feelings that we allow to creep into our minds. Exercise has been shown to be an excellent stress reducer, but you've also got to exercise your mind with positive thoughts so that you can battle the dragons of negative feelings and stress.

You have to accept that negativity is a reality and it's going to be there. A problem is in fact a *problem* until you begin to search for the potential solution, then it becomes a correction opportunity. A correction opportunity is a positive way to approach a negative situation. It's all a matter of thought and perception. If you perceive the problem as an unslayable dragon, then it's going to eat you up and you are going to have a bad day.

Some problems can't be overcome. But we've got to be smart enough to realize when we can't do anything about a situation. We must be able to recognize when it's too big, it has too much control over us and we've got to let go and get help. If the problem is insurmountable, recognize it and go on. If you can't handle it, get someone who can. Don't be afraid to ask someone for help.

Success is Shipped in Small Containers. Mediocrity is Shipped in Railroad Cars.

As the statement above says, mediocrity, unfortunately, is more commonplace than excellence. The price of mediocrity is shameful. Mediocrity is inexcusable. When you settle for mediocrity, you pay a price the rest of your life.

The biggest problem we find in business is that many executives are so tuned into their ego, they think they have nothing more to learn. They end up losing their job or taking a demotion because they don't have the qualities to do a certain task and they are too pig-headed to admit they need to ask for help. Sometimes even when they ask for help they aren't willing to follow through and learn the skills that are required to help them achieve their goals.

I once had a friend who was a chief financial officer of a company. His goal was to become CEO. The problem was, he didn't want it enough to make some changes in his work style. In his case, he needed to acquire some people skills. He and I talked often about his goals. Although he was an expert in financial matters, his ability to get along with the people he interacted with on a daily basis was limited at best. I advised him that until everyone associated with him wanted to see him become chief executive officer and until he had their admiration and respect, he wouldn't achieve his goal. I suggested ways he could acquire the skills he needed. I encouraged him to take courses that would help him improve his people skills. I explained that his associates didn't have to *like* him, but they had to believe in his abilities and respect him enough to believe he would handle the responsibilities of the position better than anyone else.

A good CEO helps everyone do their jobs better. He or she encourages them to strengthen their skills, set goals and achieve them. A good CEO is a mentor. My friend had the potential. He was intelligent. Unfortunately, he was unwilling to honestly evaluate himself, make the necessary adjustments and develop the skills required to earn the respect of his subordinates and co-workers. Needless to say, he didn't become CEO and eventually left the company.

Is failure really failure if you've done your best? Absolutely not! Failure will happen, even to successful people. Failure is when you're not willing to give it your very best and put out the effort that is required to achieve your goal.

In the movie "Rudy", a young man goes to Notre Dame to play football and manages to only make the practice squad. For four years he practices faithfully with the rest of the team. He gives it his best, but he never gets to play. Then in the final game of his senior year the coach sends him into the game. It's only for two plays, but he gets to play. Was Rudy a failure? Not in my opinion. He worked hard, and didn't give up. He wasn't a great football player, and somewhere inside he probably realized that, but he did his best. That determination and inner will made him a winner in his own right.

As a self-proclaimed (of course) authority on human behavior patterns, it is with great wisdom, insight and astute analysis that I suggest to you that many influences affect our behavior. A variety of emotions such as fear, caution or uncertainty can cause the mind to direct behavior in a less than proper or sensible manner. Selfishness and jealousy are two emotions which need to be carefully controlled.

You don't get credit for what you do. Someone else has the good luck or gets promoted. A co-worker gets recognized or complimented for something that isn't nearly as important as what you've done. What's the use of "busting your buttons" when it doesn't do any good and no one cares or appreciates you? Why do you always get the crappy assignments? You did all the work and they didn't even mention your name when they praised the accomplishment. You only got a 3% raise and they got more. They only like her because she's good looking....

These thoughts and comments are all negative and negativity is something that should be totally eliminated from your thought and behavior patterns. Negativity is a disease that festers and rots. It gets into your bloodstream and destroys your positive organisms. Negativity is overpowering and overwhelming. Positivity is refreshing and easy to live with. It reproduces rapidly and can erase all the negatives.

Certainly, things beyond your own control will sometimes contribute to you not reaching the achievements you expect.

Taking a positive stance and deciding that you will do the best with the circumstances you can control will help you set your own ambitions. If you know your limitations, then you should be able to judge your ambition level. If you want to exceed your limitations, and you can, that will come from your heart, and mind and determination.

The "$5 Job" at the beginning of the chapter is applicable to every situation we face in life. There is always an opportunity to improve. There's always a chance to perform or do a little better than you did before. The opportunity to learn and achieve is phenomenal and never ending.

If you're content with mediocre accomplishments and that's all you expect because you enjoy your life that way and everything falls in place for you, that's okay too. It all boils down to deciding what you really want. Are you tough enough, determined enough, willing to work hard enough, to achieve your goal? You may not always get to the level you desire, but if you have the right frame of mind, you will reach some level of accomplishment and success. Many people shoot for the stars. Some miss and hit the moon.

If you continue to gain knowledge, improve your skills and become good at what you do, even though today's marketplace is highly competitive, you will always be in demand as an executive or an employee.

Strive To Be The Best

You should be the kind of person who strives to be the best.
To take each day with vital nutrition, combining work with your play.
The way we generate our destination leaves us with or without our dream.
The foils and toil of each generation begins within our genes.

What is it you want to achieve as you pass through this life?
Is it mediocrity or superiority or just to pass the time?
Remember, whatever your plans may be, they must begin in your mind.
As we plant the seed and nurture it from sun to setting sun.
We'll gauge the way we've done our work, and if the battle is won.

No guarantees of end results will fall upon our feet.
Hard work you say, and I repeat, hard work rewards the feat.
Never have I been so sure of one of life's rewards,
As when I look into my eyes and know I've worked so hard.

Reality is as ever dawned if you control your time.
We lose a few by casually stopping for the rhyme.
The things we lose by chewing, chews its very valuable time.

It's easy to pass a looking glass and stop to admire the view,
Or talk about the things that passed with another one or two,
Who will gladly take the idle time to ignore the work they should be doing,
Instead of helping you, they can throw away your total being.
(OGB)

Sacrifice

The price of success is high. The price of success can be a great deal of pain. It can be a stress to your health. The price of success will cost you long hours. The price of success will cause you to concentrate on gaining knowledge and skill training until you get it right. The price of success will sometimes cause you anxiety at home. It can put unbearable pressure on your family. It can cause you to lose friends, or forfeit your social life. It can interfere with your church, community, or recreational activities. It can even result in divorce. Success can have an extremely expensive price tag. In light of the sacrifices you will have to make, what's so great about being successful? Because the price of failure is even greater. You pay for success only temporarily; you pay for failure the rest of your life.

Even though there is sacrifice involved there are benefits. There are, of course, financial rewards. But success isn't just about money. Success is about rejuvenation of your inner self. The vitality of accomplishment. The inner satisfaction of having reached a goal. To say you will and then "do it." The mental strength to make ourselves put out the effort to be the best at what we do. The consequences are far less threatening than the rewards of recognition, achievement and personal gratification that comes from being your best. The drive to be the best janitor, concert pianist, accountant, attorney, doctor, teacher, pilot or lathe operator; the drive to "be all that you can be" says it will be worth the sacrifice.

The price of success is the subject, but circumstances can also be involved. If you get started on a path of accomplishment and that path gets complicated and needs attention, you are challenged to regain control. Sometimes you get locked in because you've got your neck stuck out so far you have no choice but to keep after it and work your way out. When that happens, the goal dictates to you rather than you being able to dictate how much you can give to it. If you give less than is required, you fail. These business complications can take time away from other important things in your life, your family, friends and community service. What many people don't realize is that once you have developed a project or a company, you may not control it; it may control you. Many times you can delegate tasks to someone else, but no matter how well you delegate, unless the person you delegate to has an interest or a strong drive to succeed, or unless they have a personal stake in the business, then they will probably not always follow through and do what they should to get the job done. When they fail, the only one who can pick up the ball and run with it is you. The buck has to stop somewhere and if you don't want to see years of struggle, effort and accomplishment go down the drain, then it has to stop with you.

A Hard Worker Never Lets His or Her Guard Down, Never has a Casual Attitude About any Aspect of the Job

Don't expect to get a lot of credit for the sacrifices you make. A person who tries to have a win-win situation with family or associates at all times and at all levels is kidding themselves. It just isn't going to happen.

I made a sincere and honest effort to be at every special function or event for my family members when they were growing up. I tried to keep time open for them. I did this by shoving a lot of work into one day. If I was traveling, I'd start out early, work all day and basically squeeze a typical five-day trip into a two-day trip. I did it because it was important to me to give my family the time they needed.

Sometimes my family doesn't realize how hard I worked to be at their special events or functions. Explaining the sacrifice only sounds self-serving and no one believes it. The fact is, no matter how much "quality time" you spend with your family, it will only be quality time if it is spent with them when they want you to spend it with them. Their time schedule may be the only one they understand and if your time doesn't match their time and you're not available when **they** want you to be, you are going to be criticized.

Make Time for Things that are Important

At the risk of being inconsistent, I have to plead the case for making time for things that are important to you. Those things may be hobbies, family, friends, church or whatever. Success does come with sacrifice, but I remember someone once told me, "I never knew anybody who, on his death bed, said, 'I wish I'd spent more time at work.'"

It's all a matter of perspective. When I was a young man, senior citizens would tell me that life would be over soon and I should enjoy it while I could. Now that I'm a senior citizen I understand what they meant and I find myself telling young people the same thing.

Have you ever known someone who had experienced a life threatening situation or had someone close to them experience one? Usually this causes personalities to change.

A few years ago, I took a fishing trip with some friends. We were flying to our destination, as a group, in two older model twin engine airplanes. The trip was plagued by weather delays and one of these delays forced us to stay overnight in Del Rio, Texas. Early the next morning, we took off. As the plane I was in became airborne, I looked out the window at the ground below and was horrified to see the second plane crash on take-off.

We immediately returned to the field. We rushed over to the demolished remains of the second plane. Fortunately, there were only minor injuries among our friends. However, each of those individuals was changed forever. They now look at life in an entirely different manner. Their priorities are not the same.

What am I trying to say here? Do the best you can to make time for the important things in your life, and keep these things, as much as possible, separate from your business life. The simple things in life truly are often the most rewarding. Stopping to smell a rose may not produce a life changing event, but it may cause you to realize that children grow up quickly, time rushes past, we are in this life a relatively short period of time, and you need to take time to enjoy it.

Confidentiality

I can't stress enough the importance of confidentiality. We've all heard the military saying "Loose lips sink ships." In many cases, you can gain advancement or attention by your ability to be a confidant and keep information to yourself.

People love to gossip and talk about others, especially in the workplace. Very few people in today's workplace know how to keep a confidence. It can become a big factor in your success and it is something you need to give serious thought.

It's always been important to me to not to betray a person's confidence. When I was a youngster, Arawana, my cousin, lived with us because her parents had died. She used to take me to the movies. Sometimes she let a boy walk her home from the theater. Of course, I was with them and she knew my mother wouldn't approve of her walking with a boy. She would say to me, "Don't you tell on me," and I never did. I learned at that young age that confidentiality was something that would gain respect and admiration.

Sadly, trust is often broken. You know how it goes. You tell your best friend a secret and ask, "Please, don't tell anybody." Then, they in turn have a confidential discussion with someone they trust and say, "Now, I'm going to tell you this, but don't tell anyone else." By the time the story is multiplied, it might as well have been printed in the newspaper.

There's more at stake than personal betrayal when you are asked to keep a business confidence. Breaking a confidence in business situations can have legal ramifications. Breaking a confidence can destroy a business negotiation.

If you're known as a person who can be trusted to keep a business confidence, your superiors and business colleagues will have a tremendous amount of respect for you. Trust is not-negotiable. You must trust the people with whom you deal each day and they must trust you.

Beware of gossip! The amount of gossip I've encountered in my life is staggering. Stories about me have been astronomical, both about my business and personal life. Half truths, untruths, innuendoes and outright fabrications have been in some cases bizarre. Many have been vicious, unreasonable and uncomplimentary, but mostly they have been untrue and unwarranted. Be aware that the price of success is also being the target of gossip.

The Harder You Work, the More You're Worth

No matter where you live, regardless of your geographic area or how complex the labor market is, regardless of what is going to be required to get a job in the 21st century, there will always be a demand for good employees. An employee who is reliable, productive, honest, efficient, organized, cordial and pleasant while doing their job will always be in demand no matter how constrained the current job market may be.

The hard work ethic seems to have changed a great deal over the last 50 years. Many people today think they are "owed" a job because they have a certain degree or because they know someone influential.

The fact is, the 21st century job market is going to be very demanding and competitive. It's already getting that way. It will be tougher to find a job that pays good money, provides benefits and the other compensations that people have come to expect.

Hard work is imperative if you are going to start a business and hard work is a must if you want to have a good job. If you work your job, and gain the knowledge and skills that increase your value to your employer, you will be in demand because you are a productive asset to any employer. You must be a doer. The quest for knowledge and personal improvement is a daily routine among doers.

Where do you look to see the way of your future? I suggest the mirror!

2
Like the Little Engine That Could...

Remember the childhood story about the little engine that made it up the hill by saying, "I think I can, I think I can?" In order to have any kind of success you need to have the self-esteem and the confidence to believe that you can get the job done. Just like the little engine, your inner will must be strong and ready for the test.

As you approach your long-term goals and plans, remember that all things need to be considered. Think of what you need to do, what you have to do, and, most importantly, what you **want** to do.

What is Self-Confidence?

Self-confidence is the ability to believe in your own capabilities to function and accomplish your goals. If you think you can, you can. If you think you can't, you won't.

The first step in doing anything is having the confidence before you start that you can do it. If you start out to run a mile, and you try to look at the end, it looks like a long way. You'll probably be tempted to think you can't do it. However, if you say, "I'll just take this challenge as far as I can, and I'll only look at one block at a time," the perspective changes. When you get to the end of the first block, you probably will think, "Hey, I can go another one." By the second block you might be hurting and those negative thoughts of "I can't" start coming into your head. You will be able to think of a thousand excuses and reasons to stop and rest but that's the exact moment when you find out how strong your self-confidence and determination are. Can you go that extra block or more? If you truly want to you can.

The truth is that we can, and are able to do more if we believe in ourselves. Our minds can be taught to convince us that we're stronger than we think, we're smarter than we think, in fact, we're able to do just about anything we set our minds to.

Because I Believe In Me

Because I believe in me, I am strong.
Because I believe in me, I will win.
Because I believe in me, I know I must work.
Because I believe in me, I will learn.
Because I believe in me, I will be better.
Because I believe in me, I will always be proud of me.

Learning About Yourself

Ironically, in the process of training your mind, you learn something about yourself as a person. Maybe you don't make the mile the first time. But you don't give up. You try it again another time, and you get a little farther. You try again and this time you make it! You have to battle the same thoughts each time. The same reasons for quitting are there. But you're building upon small successes, and in turn, your confidence builds.

First one mile, then two, and who knows from there! To face the negatives and win against the desire to give up is a combination of self-confidence and knowing that you can accomplish difficult objectives.

Small objectives can turn into marathons. There is no one on this earth that got up one day and said, "I believe I can run a 26 mile marathon today," and then went out and did it. Twenty-six miles and 385 yards or only one block non-stop all begin the same. One foot in front of the other, always extending yourself a little further and a little further until you've covered the ground and seen the end. The finished mechanism of success, knowing and feeling your accomplishment, comes from the head, the heart and the development of yourself.

The inner strength in us is sometimes unrecognized because of our personalities and demeanor. I lost a niece, Patty, to cancer this year. A nephew, Gary, died in 1986 from the same disease. The way they reacted positively to life while facing death was so uplifting to me. Patty always had a positive attitude and was so courageous that she was an inspiration to all of us. Her sister, Dellena, has multiple sclerosis and is in a wheelchair, but she is also always positive. She handles her affliction with a pleasant, congenial attitude. Another niece, Dena, was born with cerebral palsy and has never let it be a concern to her. She leads a positive and full life with two grown children and a grandchild. All of my family members, including children, nieces, nephews and cousins, are a positive influence and inspiration to me each day. They all possess a confidence in themselves and have used that confidence to overcome or deal with what some people may consider tragic conditions.

I try to remember the old adage, "I used to complain because I had no shoes, until I saw the person with no feet." I try to walk in another's moccasins before I condemn or criticize.

Love is a gender
Love outlives hate
Love last forever
If only we wait
And not overreact
To the sudden impulse
And go off the handle
Without just cause

Don't burn bridges or think that you're the only one who's misunderstood or who got a bum rap. Life is like a game of cards; some get all good cards, some mixed, and some bad ones. Make the most you can out of your hand.

Self-confidence is having a positive mind-set and should be a part of your life. There is, of course, the inherent danger of being so self-confident that you become unrealistic about your capabilities. You can be overconfident and nonsensical in approaching reality.

Teenagers are a perfect example. There is something about the teenage years that is a true paradox. Teenagers think they're adults. They want free rein to do what they want, when they want, with whom they want, for as long as they want! They want to date or go steady and will fight with their parents for the right to do so. Their favorite rationale is: "Everyone else is doing it." If given this unrestrained freedom they usually get into stressful situations that they do not yet have the maturity to handle. Peer pressure can lead them into many unacceptable practices such as drinking, drugs and sex. If allowed to date the same boy or girl regularly they generally spend a great deal of unsupervised time with that person and being normal red-blooded teenagers they make decisions that are not controlled by their brain. Common sense, logic and practicality are not the guidelines in these circumstances.

These young people often make decisions they know are wrong or unacceptable. They place themselves smack in the middle of frustration, anxiety and mental stress because they know what they are doing isn't right. The pressure they impose on themselves is often unbearable resulting in depression, a damaged self-esteem, or in a few cases they convince themselves that it's okay for them to continue to do what they're doing. Sooner or later, however, they come to the realization that they are trying to deal with situations that they are not equipped to deal with.

These years are the time when children and young adults would really prefer to be told what they can and can't do and then be held accountable for their actions. They need some guidelines and boundaries. This takes away the pressure of making decisions they're not ready to make on their own. Part of parenting is being able to take the "blame" for making them different from all their friends. They may say they "hate" you during this time of their life, but somewhere deep down inside they know they are loved, and that their parents are trying to do what's best for them. I've often heard it said, "When I was 18 I thought my parents were the stupidest people in the world so I left home. When I returned at 21 it was amazing how much they had learned in three years." Where in the world could they get that much knowledge? By the time I was 30, my parents had become geniuses! Well, almost.

The point is, overconfidence can lead to putting yourself "out on a limb" by causing expectations to become failures. So at least listen to what others, including your parents, are trying to tell you.

Reality Versus Self-Confidence

A thin line separates reality from self-confidence; much like a thin line separates a genius from a moron. We need to know our limitations and yet continually raise our standards, based on self-improvement, gained knowledge, skills, attitude and habits.

Qualify what you can do by laying out a plan for how you are going to do it. The self-confidence comes from the performance of each step you take to get there.

"I'm going to become a supervisor by being the best operator in the company. I'm going to become a superintendent by being the best supervisor in the company. I'm going to become a vice-president by being the most knowledgeable, intuitive and best prepared, sense-of-urgency person in the company. I'm going to become president because of my colleagues' respect for me and the good and positive things I've accomplished along the way."

Outline each of these ambitions ahead of time. Then work your plan and as you go continue to show a hunger for knowledge and a burning desire to learn all that you can. It will become obvious that you're not there to just "get by."

Our level of confidence is determined by a mental attitude set forth in either a positive mind-set; a negative mind-set; or no mind-set. You can learn the effects of each of these mind-sets by observing other people. Their mind-set will also reflect their desire, their expectations, why they're even doing what they are doing with their lives. We can learn a lot from people around us by asking them to tell us a way that we could improve to make us be received better by people with whom we come in contact. If they are honest with you, they will usually tell you something they have noticed in your mannerisms that they don't like. Unfortunately, we all have habits and traits that are offensive to someone. We don't even realize we're being perceived negatively. **Caution:** Make sure that you can take the comments or criticism objectively. It's not a good idea to be defensive when you're hearing something about yourself that you don't want to hear, especially if you've asked for it!

The person who lacks the ability to believe in herself as much or more than anyone else in the world, even her parents, relegates herself to carrying a doubt around about her ambition and vision to be in the upper levels of achievement. Isn't it pitiful to see a person have so little regard for her abilities that she sets her goals lower than what she could accomplish with determination and commitment?

Our mind-set is often stimulated from the confidence instilled in us by our parents or environment as we grow up. Many children are restricted or stifled by parents who are too strict with them. These parents never allow their children the opportunity to explore their individuality. Our personalities need to be expressed openly in various and numerous ways. Parents should guide and direct their children's emerging personalities and, as we said earlier, they may even need to control their children's activities to an extent, but they should never suppress these fragile emerging personalities.

The workplace is no different. Personalities and ideas need to be cultivated and encouraged. We need to know what's inside the people with whom we work. An out-going personality will communicate eagerly. A laid-back or introverted personality may require some encouragement. We, therefore, have to learn the difference. We must view our employees and associates the same way a coach surveys his or her players; evaluate their strengths and challenges and then place them where they can produce the best results.

Developing the perfect work environment is an ongoing challenge, especially with the changing attitudes of workers. What we give and take may be expected, but little appreciated. Happy is different things to different people and to some borders on the ridiculous.

Success Requires Cooperation, Communication, and an Inter-Exchange of Information From all Parties

The value of self-confidence, well defined and realistic, is that you can be more effective. It will allow you to deal with yourself from different perspectives. It will also allow you to take a broader and more flexible perspective of each issue or situation you encounter. At the same time you will be developing mutual respect among your peers and fellow workers. You should have a systematic and balanced confidence level mentally, physically and socially. You will feel good about your decisions, suggestions and personal habits. You will become more proactive, assertive (not aggressive) and respond to challenges directly and confidently.

While walking down the street I ran into a friend.

"Hi, where are you headed?", he asked.

"I'm just going to Ned's funeral."

"Is Ned dead?"

"No, he just thought he'd have his funeral and get it out of the way."

Stupid questions are asked every day. Don't be *reactive,* be *proactive!*

Our minds control our every move, and confidence is always helpful. However, don't forget that all of us together can accomplish a whole lot more than one of us isolated.

Know When to be Humble

When you've done something special or accomplished a feat; when you've excelled in some way, it is okay to feel proud of what you've done. You've probably worked very hard to accomplish the task. But, beware of "tooting your own horn." The words "I" and "me" can create resentment in others. The words "we" and "us" sound better. If you've done something truly worthy of recognition, someone will notice and talk about it. If you think you are smart, let someone else say so. Your accomplishment will sound better coming from someone else. Third party compliments are much more powerful than those expressed by ourselves.

Bob Wilson, a friend of mine, has a great sense of humor. One time a group of us were playing golf when Tom Murphy, another friend and member of the group, said, "Bob, I hear you had a hole in one on this course?"

Bob didn't say anything. I looked at him and asked, "Did you have a hole in one?"

He still didn't say anything, and I pushed him further. "Oh come on Bob, did you have a hole in one?"

He just shrugged his shoulders and grinned and said, "Hasn't everybody?"

That's the kind of attitude I like!

Remember too, the feeling of self-importance can be shattered easily. There is always someone who can outdo us. So, let's not judge ourselves <u>great</u> until others have confirmed it. Then, let your goal become helping someone else do it better or accomplish even more that you have. The true test of the heart is finding the reward in helping others succeed.

3
The Most Valuable Asset

"Use your head."

"Just think about it."

"Now, doesn't that just make sense?"

How many times have you heard these comments throughout your life? I've heard them plenty and I've said them almost as often.

We can probably sum up the secret to success by using our most valuable asset when making business decisions - common sense. When we use logic and reason to make logical, as opposed to illogical, decisions we are using common sense. It's as simple as knowing that you can't cross a busy intersection with 50 cars whizzing through it. It's as simple as knowing not to stand closely behind a horse.

Most people have some level of common sense because of their life experiences. They've gone through their life making certain decisions and enjoying the benefits and suffering the consequences of those decisions. These experiences have given them some level of common sense.

What happens, then, to some people to make them act illogically? They let their emotions get in the way of making good decisions. When emotions get involved in decision making, you lose the edge of common sense.

To make successful business decisions, an entrepreneur must rely on practicality, logic AND common sense. Emotion is a large part of our personal life because of our loved ones and our friends. But in business, the bottom line is the driving factor in decision making and it is imperative that you keep emotions at arm's length as much as possible.

For example, I sometimes feel as if I have two personalities-one for my personal life and one for my business life. In my personal life I think I'm a very generous man. But in business, I want every penny accounted for.

While emotion has a great deal to do with common sense, intelligence often has very little to do with it. I have spent a career in the financial world and as an economist. I know many professional people who are very intelligent in their chosen field. I have seen countless doctors, lawyers and other very successful professional people make an unbelievable mess of their personal finances. They try to invest or capitalize on their retirement moneys without seeking advice from a financial expert. Many of these same people wouldn't think of making a business decision without consulting someone else, but when it comes to their personal finances they make decisions completely out of their educational background. That's not using common sense.

I must admit that common sense alone won't insure economic success. But it is a vital ingredient to any kind of business venture. Common sense must be applied from the beginning. It is what guides the decision of what kind of business venture you will have and where to locate it.

I have a Common Sense Guideline that I use when making my business decisions.

1. What are the consequences of this decision?
2. Who will be affected by these decisions?
3. How will I correct the situation if the process develops negatively?
4. What's the picture look like long-term?
5. Do I have all the facts to make this decision?

If I can answer these five questions to my satisfaction when making a decision, then I feel comfortable proceeding.

4
Nothing Stays the Same

Our society is constantly changing. You cannot deny it, you cannot fight it. The best you can do is work with it, finding opportunity in the change itself. Accepting change as a given will help you develop flexible programs for your company and a flexible personality for yourself. What some people call business intuition is really a way of looking at a business situation and knowing that change is inevitable. You must always expect and be prepared for change.

The last hundred years have brought many changes to society as a whole, but especially to the American way of life. It is truly mind boggling to consider some of these changes and then to look toward what the future holds in the next 100 years!

Before 1895, automobiles were only in the inventive stage. Now, one hundred years later, those first, slow moving automobiles, that needed to be cranked up from outside the vehicle in order to run, have matured into sophisticated machines complete with computerized ignition systems and voices that tell you when you need gas, digital indicators that tell you the outside weather, and in some race cars, the ability to travel at more than 300 miles an hour.

One hundred years ago, the only way to travel was by horse, or horse and wagon. If you wanted to go to a foreign country, you did so by boat. The Wright brothers' invention of the airplane caused a dramatic change in our mode of travel. As they were fashioning their simple craft, I wonder if they realized that their "invention" would launch not only a remarkable mode of transportation but an incredibly competitive industry. From an assemblage of ash wood, cloth and steel wires to small prop-engines, to super-sonic jets capable of breaking the sound barrier and vehicles used to explore outer space. All in just one hundred years! Just think about it, from Kitty Hawk to the moon, in only 100 years!

Turn-of-the-century medicine was simplistic at best. We treated illnesses with herbs, roots and natural home remedies. Anesthesia was still in the experimental stages; surgical instruments were primitive by comparison. If an individual lived to be sixty, they were old. To say that medical science in the 1890's was unsophisticated compared to today is certainly an understatement. I'm not even sure that organ transplants and replacements were even thoughts in someone's head one hundred years ago. Now, advanced technology is making the transplanting of organs from one human to another almost routine. Where will that technology take us in the future? It has already increased an individual's life expectancy by over twenty years. The increase in life expectancy will dramatically affect the business world. People over the next one hundred years may not be ready to retire at 65, and maybe not even at 70. What changes will that have on our society as a whole? Are we, as entrepreneurs and business owners looking toward how we can utilize this increasing labor pool? We'd better be if we hope to remain competitive!

Not all of the changes over the past century have been positive. Some have created more problems than they have solved. The social changes that occurred as a result of the Great Depression are a perfect example. When Franklin Delano Roosevelt took office in 1932, this country was in a tragic state. People were standing in soup lines and just trying to get by. Living conditions weren't all that great for most of America. Banks were failing, jobs were almost impossible to find and when you found one, they barely paid enough to provide the necessities. FDR installed social programs, work programs, the WPA and other benefits that would eventually put this country back on its feet. But some of those programs have been so abused that now, some sixty years later, they have created some very serious problems for this and future generations. Some of these programs are why we have a deficit budget and overspending by our government.

One of the best examples of this is the Social Security program. The program was originally designed to provide enough money to help people with subsistence needs during their retirement years. But it became a political football and more and more people were added to the list of those to be helped. The cost of the program grew. The fund became actuarially unsound, because instead of being saved for the people who were paying into the program, it was being used to pay for those claiming benefits today. Many people have drawn social security who have paid very little into it. Now as we grow older in this generation, we see that it is going to be difficult for us to ever collect what we have paid into the program over our lifetime. The SSA is finding more and more ways to restrict your ability to draw your funds. Realistically, it is your money; you paid into it and you should be entitled to that annuity, that benefit, that retirement program, regardless of what you make in earnings. The larger question is, "Will future generations get anything?" Will our grandchildren be willing to continue to pay for the social security benefits that we're supposed to receive? It's doubtful. So you can see, that although these social programs eased the crisis in the 30's, they are causing more and more crisis in the 90's and beyond.

Another example of a social program gone awry is the current welfare system. It has become a cancer on our society. From one generation to another, some welfare recipients are literally sucking the blood out of our revenues because they are getting something for nothing.

Some other areas that desperately need change and realignment are the military build-up, the cost of foreign aid, military weaponry and space exploration. All of these factors have placed a huge burden on the federal budget. Naturally, some of these should not be overlooked and they should not be reduced. They should always be a part of our consideration for spending money, but within reason.

It is my belief that we need to begin immediately to deal with the decline in our moral values, the increase in the use of drugs, the increase in crime and welfare and the ecological laws and programs that we have installed which are all major contributors to our ever-growing national debt. Additional concerns are trade deficits, allowing other countries to cause huge trade deficits, the technological explosions that have taken place and the high property values that the technology companies have been able to receive. All these factors are areas that need a great deal of consideration. Yes, the next 100 years are definitely something to be concerned about as we try to find solutions to these problems.

People, such as my father and his father, didn't have the "essentials" we have today. My parents lived in the country and their closest neighbor was five miles away. They raised their own meat, milked their own cows and their source of cash was cutting down trees to make into railroad ties. These were sold for 50 cents each. They made $.75 to $1.00 a day and that was all they needed. They used kerosene lamps because they had no electricity. They had outdoor bathroom facilities and their water was from a well they dug by hand. They bathed, usually on Saturday night, in a Number 2 tub behind the pot-belly stove. Water for the bath was heated on the stove. They had a lot of kids, and that bathtub didn't get fresh water with every kid. It wasn't the most enjoyable environment, especially if you were the last kid, but then, they didn't have as many worries as we do today, either.

A single discovery or invention can change the way all succeeding generations live. That's what happened in my parents' case. When coal or other natural resources were discovered in an area, mines were dug and many people-my parents included-left their rural homes for the mining camps. Working for a mining company in those days was very different from today. The protections for the employee and the environment didn't exist. Working hours weren't restricted and the employer could and did exploit their workers and the land. The pay was meager and what money the miners got went back to the "Company Store", where they had to shop. These unfair practices, of course, eventually led to organized labor and the creation of unions.

That's how this country evolved. People went where they could find work. We see a different type of evolution happening today. Major industries are cutting back, down-sizing or shutting down. Our labor-intensive industries are shrinking, causing displaced employees with little or no skills to compete in the more service-industry type jobs that are taking labor's place. This is a change for which many workers have not been prepared.

Success comes when individuals or companies envision change and then capitalize on it.

Really think about the evolutions and revolutions that have occurred in our country over the years. Let's take one specific example-television. Before the 1950's, TV wasn't available. Actually, many homes didn't even have radios, and television was barely in the planning stages. In 1953, the television set became a household commodity for almost everyone in the country. The businesses that acknowledged this change and pondered the way it could and would change our society capitalized on the change and made a good deal of money in the process. Other companies, who failed to recognize the coming changes were passed by.

The great Atlantic & Pacific Tea Company is a great example. This company had its own sugar and coffee plantations, canneries and bakeries. They were totally integrated. There were A & P grocery stores all over the country. They were the number one food supplier.

Along came television and the opportunity to advertise. Many companies saw the opportunity; A & P didn't. They didn't believe that people would watch television commercials and come to believe that Stokely, and Van Camp's, were a better brand of canned goods than their own Ann Page, brand. They also didn't believe television commercials would change the public's opinion on coffee brands, that Folgers, and Maxwell House, would become more popular than their own Eight O'Clock, fresh ground brand. They didn't believe that local bakery bread would sell better or that other brands of sugar would be more appealing. A & P didn't prepare for the future or capitalize on an opportunity and they were outmarketed. Where are they today? Oh, they're still around, but they are a much smaller, scaled down company. They no longer dominate the retail grocery industry and mainly because they didn't accept change.

A more positive example of change is the university I attended. When I was there it was called Kansas State Teachers College. There were 1100 students, no dorms, no student union, no technology center, and an old run-down gym which was on the second floor of one of the buildings. The campus was essentially confined to a few buildings; most of which were old and run-down. Veterans on the G.I. Bill were a dominant presence on the campus. These GIs dictated attitudes in many cases and their maturity and behavior were imposed on their younger classmates. I was 16 or 17 and interacted with the older adults. I learned a great deal from the experience. It could have been negative. Drinking, partying, class skipping and poor study habits could have dominated. For me, it didn't. I was paying for my own education and that made me want to get full value. Ambition made me want to succeed and compete in everything I did.

Today this university has about 6,500 students; many new buildings and renovations. A student union, a new gym, planetarium, new social science building, dorms-men's and women's, it's own radio station, and a new state-of-the-art technology center. This center will be one of the top 4 or 5 in the country and will increase enrollment which will increase development in the community and that in turn will benefit the entire state.

There are any number of instances where changes in the business world have caused one time "giants" to become less dominant in the marketplace. Look at IBM, Sears and J.C. Penney. Only in very small communities do you ever see a Western Auto store, but at one time they were the place to buy auto parts. If you want to stay on top, be more aware of what is five years ahead than what tomorrow holds.

The success of any business venture depends upon its leader's vision. It is essential that you, as a leader, develop a perspective on change. It's the ability to construct that vision that establishes you on the ladder to success. Change causes change.

Transformation is Controlled Change

Change will occur. By being aware of it and prepared for it, we can take charge of change. One way to be prepared is to stay current. The need to keep current on what's happening in several businesses and be well informed on different business segments and industries challenges me to continually seek education on these matters. I try to impress and surprise my associates by showing them I know the business and what's going on. One associate told another that I really didn't understand the business (one of our entities.) When you give birth to something, and breast feed it into success, believe me, "you know the business." It may change and you may temporarily fall behind times but if you're smart, you stay updated. You don't have to broadcast your efforts but it's nice to express your up-datedness at unexpected times. It raises a few surprised eyebrows. It's fun, too!

Realize, however, that you cannot completely control change. There are some changes too powerful to be controlled. Again, you must be flexible. You also must be intuitive.

Intuition is Being Ready for Change

Intuition, as it relates to success, is having the ability to perceive change. Change can mean a negative course or a positive course for a business. Successful leaders find ways to make change take a positive course for their business.

As we saw in the example of the A & P grocery chain, somebody didn't have the intuition to perceive the change brought on by mass media. A & P passed up an opportunity to stay on top of its competitors.

The founders of Pizza Hut, Frank and Dan Carney, saw the opportunity behind an Italian dish consisting of dough, tomato sauce, spices, cheese and a variety of toppings. Until 1958, pizza had been more of a specialty item found mainly in large cities. The Carneys realized that pizza was fairly easy and inexpensive to make and one pie could feed a whole family. They believed pizza was a food product that could be mass produced and sold for an inexpensive price. It could also be a snack or filler food. That was the idea behind the Pizza Hut company.

The idea came at a time when the country was booming and more and more families were eating out. The brothers Carney perceived a change, saw an opportunity and took it!

Before I bought my first Pizza Hut franchise, I had only had pizza twice in my life; once in Chicago's Beltloops and once while I was at summer camp in the military. I liked it both times. I did have pizza one other time, in Topeka, and as I bit into the pie, it burned the top of my mouth. I didn't realize pizzas were cooked at 550°.

Pizza Hut is now the largest pizza company in the world! NPC International, Inc. is the largest franchisee. It's a different climate today. Pizza is now a common food item. It may not be a good idea to start a new pizza franchise company because the market is so fragmented. However, many people still enter the pizza business every year and some are successful.

Remember, transformation is controlled change. Think again about the changes that have occurred in the last 100 years. Put them into perspective as to what they may mean for the next 100 years.

Some changes have had a ripple effect in advancing our society. Before we had automobiles, the mode of transportation was horse and buggy. The invention of the automobile helped our society move about the land, exploring new frontiers. The airplane made it easier for us to journey to new worlds and observe new cultures. The advent of the space program has allowed us to envision travel to other planets and perhaps even other solar systems.

Advances in medical science have made it possible to live longer, healthier, more productive lives. We can transplant human organs and, one day, we'll be able to manufacture artificial organs successfully.

The computer has and continues to change our society. Remember the first computer was housed in two skyscrapers. The first units were available only to large businesses and very expensive. Today they are a common item in many homes and small enough to be carried in a case no larger than a briefcase. With the development of the "Internet" and "World Wide Web" the entire world is interconnected. I believe these will soon be outdated systems through the advancement of new technologies.

I can assure you that because of transformation the cultures of the world will begin to be more and more like each other. Religious beliefs, taboos and other practices will always separate us to some degree but we'll share the same type of food, same type of entertainment, sports and other activities.

When you think of the next 100 years, think of the interaction that will be taking place because of the rapid advancement in technology. What successes will prevail because of our intuition, our ability to perceive and even predict change, and then be in a position to capitalize on it? What new companies and businesses will spring up in anticipation of these changes? The Internet is providing new ground for all kinds of ideas, just as television provided opportunities in the 1950's.

This is what I mean by intuition. Changes will occur down the line, but you must be intuitive enough to be in a position to capitalize on that change.

Intuitive people aren't procrastinators. They have a sense of urgency. They live and thrive in the here and NOW!

Sense of Urgency

Most people can relate to times in high school or college when they had a deadline to meet, a paper to write or daily homework to complete. Then something would come along that was a lot more fun than those responsibilities. Maybe friends wanted to go out partying or see a movie. The temptation can be strong to put off our responsibilities for something more enjoyable.

We live in a daily struggle between doing the things that we have to do and the things we want to do. A change in perspective can help overcome these temptations. Instead of saying we "have to" do something, it's a lot more productive to say we "get to" do something. Also, remember procrastination will only make tomorrow more stressful.

Successful people who started with a goal or vision have acquired this "sense of urgency" when confronting tasks or challenges. They know that by "getting to" do these things, they are furthering their success and achievements.

I used to tell my students that if they committed 40 hours a week to their education, they would never get behind, they would always be prepared and complete their projects on time. That 40 hours would include classroom time, prep time and study time. I also told them if they looked on their education as a job they would make good grades, stay on top of the power curve and work with a clear head. "After all," I asked them, "Wouldn't you be working 40 hours if you weren't in college?"

When you get behind and have to catch up, that's a negative thought in your mind and it builds stress. By keeping in a proactive mode instead of reactive mode, you can keep a clear mind and be ready to take on additional responsibilities or new challenges when they present themselves.

You can be ready for change.

Remember, There are No Problems, Only Correction Opportunities

When we say we have a problem, that immediately puts us in a negative frame of mind. After all, a problem is a puzzle, dilemma or uncertainty. Our nature is to put off problems, stay away from them, don't face them. Even the word "problem" has a negative connotation.

But, if we say we have a "correction opportunity," that puts a different light on the subject. After all, an "opportunity" is a privilege or freedom. That's a much more positive inference. It's back to the "get to" principle. It's a lot nicer to think about opportunities instead of problems.

Plan Your Work, Work Your Plan

A friend of mine once said, "Plan your work, and work your plan." The idea was nothing new. It was one of the first things I learned in business, but I had never heard the idea expressed so well.

You can find a million excuses for not doing something. You can claim to be as busy as you want to be, and you can procrastinate all you want, but those who achieve the most are those who are the busiest. If something is important to you, no matter how busy you claim to be, you'll find a way to get it done.

Most people who claim to be "too busy" are just disorganized. They have not regimented their work time. They have not prioritized their work. Don't fool yourself. Assess yourself honestly. You can fool others, but you gain nothing by fooling yourself. If you find yourself saying that you're too busy, write down what you have done that day, accounting for every portion of the hour. If you find wasted time, it's time to organize.

Write It Down

I encourage everyone, either first thing in the morning, or even better, the night before, to write down what they're going to do the next day. Write it down in order of priority, and if something comes along that is more important than what's scheduled, insert it in its order of priority. My plan for a day might look something like this:

1. 8 am   conference with key committee
2. 9 am   production or planning meeting
3. open mail
4. necessary phone calls (review reports, discussions with sales, marketing, finance)
5. working lunch - board room bankers
6. conference call with brokers/reps
7. employee productivity review (expense reports)
8. new product development (R&D)
9. engineer & design meeting
10. (variances) field trips to visit customers, suppliers, inspect and observe field operations

Because of my involvement in a variety of businesses, I have many interruptions and "spur of the moment" reactions. My planning of priority lists from day to day varies greatly. But, having my day planned before it starts still allows me to be more productive.

If I receive a phone call or other message that something more important needs attention, I insert the information in its priority order. For instance:

"Call from president to follow up on delivery correction opportunity (insert between 3 and 4)."

Sometimes things that are important to us aren't placed in a priority position because something else has to be done first. We all have priorities of commitment, priorities of due dates and priorities of our own desires.

It is simple to keep a list of priorities. In fact, most successful business people have done this. Sometimes, for one reason or another, they have quit. (Remember, "It worked so well, I quit doing it?") If you consistently practice this important form of planning and scheduling, you'll find yourself getting much more done and staying ahead of the competition. You'll find you have a clear head and can think positively about what's happening with your business. Your intuition will be sharper and you'll be better prepared for change.

It's All a Matter of Time Management

When you think about it, doesn't it just make good sense? We can achieve more if we have a sense of urgency about our work, keep a positive open mind to change, and schedule our day in a way to get the most work done. By managing our time wisely, we can get everything done that we need to get done and still have time for family and recreation. Time management is the key. If you control your time well, you are charting a course for success.

PART II

LOOKING WITHIN

1
Make Yourself Better

Power, control, or position have different effects on people. Some people automatically change. They let the power go to their heads and become self-important, domineering, and egotistical. In their own mind, they place themselves above others and are quite happy to stay on their perch; never learning, never seeing, never envisioning how they themselves can do their own job better. They're too busy telling everyone else in the company or organization how to do *their* jobs.

Then there are others who can take the responsibility and consider it a privilege to do the work or have the power they have. They understand that the further they go in business, the more others have contributed to their success. They treat others with respect and admiration. They understand that how associates do their job or handle their responsibilities reflects on their leadership and vision. Although they may have many qualities that they can teach others, they are still willing to be taught, as well.

Truly visionary people are willing to learn from others, to work at making themselves better. These leaders have a vision or a goal to work toward. They are willing to look within themselves to see how they can change and adapt to new situations and face new challenges.

The next few chapters will talk about how to improve areas of our business and personal lives. Self-improvement is essential in business because, like we've said before, everything changes. Nothing stays the same. If we fail to continually appraise ourselves and how we do business, or how we act in our personal lives, we're going to be left behind.

There are five key areas which all of us must continually work to improve: self-analysis, communication skills, listening skills, gaining knowledge, and ego-checking.

2
Self-Analysis – Be Honest With Yourself

"When I woke up this morning with no way to hold my head that didn't hurt, and the beer I had for breakfast wasn't bad, so I had one more for dessert. I stumbled through my closet and found my cleanest dirty shirt..."

Those lyrics of this old song make a point. We need to recognize our faults, weaknesses and bad habits and admit to them. If we can be honest with ourselves, look in the mirror and see reality, and not make excuses, we'll find ways to improve. Even if you're at 95% perfection, there's still room for improvement.

The point of self-analysis is to be truthful with yourself. As long as you're lying to yourself, you're missing an opportunity to do better. Eventually, even though you may not want to admit it, everyone else will also know the truth and you'll look exactly like you are, a procrastinator.

A good example of this truth is the golfer who goes out to the course to play a round. He misses a two-foot putt. He puts the ball back and does it over again, but doesn't count that first putt in his score. He lands the ball in a bad spot and decides to hit a second ball. When he's all done, he counts his best score. He says he's about a 7 handicap, when the truth of the matter is, that if he counted those exceptions he made, he's about a 12 or 13 handicap. When he goes to a tournament claiming a 7 handicap, he can't play up to his handicap because it's not a true handicap. In private play he can fool himself, but in tournament play the truth comes out. You can't really consider yourself as successful as you want to be as long as you keep making excuses along the way.

So...self-analysis boils down to honesty, integrity, a desire to better yourself and a willingness to accept constructive criticism. It's a willingness to take in information, opinions and perceptions. You have to sift through what's real and what's not, what's constructive and destructive, and still come out of it with a positive mindset.

Oh to be as Honest as a Nine-Year Old...

Have you ever noticed how perceptive children can be? I learned long ago not to try to put anything over on a kid. They'll nail you every time.

I've always had a good relationship with children. I think it's because I don't talk down to children. I try to treat them, as I do adults, with respect and dignity. After all, the only difference between a child and an adult is that an adult has had more experience. Just because children haven't had the experiences we adults have, doesn't mean they don't have opinions, feelings and dreams.

So, it was with great honor that I accepted the invitation from a very special fourth grader, Christen, to come to her class and speak. I was running for governor of Kansas at the time and Christen asked me to come to her school in Topeka. She is a sweetheart, and I couldn't turn her down.

When I went to the school, the teachers had arranged for all three fourth-grade classes to come to the school library to listen to the "speaker." It was a big deal to the children for a candidate for governor to talk to their classes. I sat in a little chair while all 80 fourth graders scattered around the floor of the library.

As a grandfather of 16, I know what a challenge it is to hold a child's attention; their attention span is only as long as their interest. You have to be creative and interesting. So, I talked to them about what a governor does and why it's important for children their age to be interested in government. I also spent time listening to their points of view and asking them questions.

I was very impressed with their knowledge of the branches of government and the responsibility of each of those branches. I asked them who the President of the United States is, and they answered in unison. I asked what the President's wife's name is, and again they all knew it was Hillary. I asked if he was a good President, and they again answered in unison.

We also spent time talking about their goals and dreams. I asked them what they wanted to grow up to be. Their answers ranged from police officer, firefighter, lawyer, doctor, athletes, you name it.

We talked about famous people and history; we talked about government and current events. They were well informed and they had some interesting insights on current events. Some children spoke bluntly and honestly about what they believe is wrong with our government and what should be changed. They spoke about their fears and they talked about their dreams.

I came away from that experience with a new respect for our future generations and a determination to try to do what I can to improve our nation and quality of life. I also came away with a determination to view my business and political dealings with new insight. Those kids have fresh minds, fresh ideas and a certain quality of innocence and trust that we lose when we get older. Oh, how I wish we didn't lose these qualities.

If I could perform magic and turn all adults into fourth graders, we might see some real honesty and improvement in the way we conduct our businesses and our politics. We most likely would make substantial progress in solving some of the problems that have plagued our country for years.

When you explain to a fourth grader the perils of the United States continuously living beyond its means and layering debt upon debt upon debt, they understand the problem and they reasonably wonder why we adults, who are so smart, don't take action to fix it.

We can all learn from our children. We need to respect those qualities of honesty and compassion and embrace them in our daily lives. Seeing the world through the eyes of a child is refreshing. Some of our government leaders could improve themselves greatly by placing themselves in front of a fourth-grade class.

Self-Analysis is not Second Guessing

All of us have made some kind of mistake at one time or another. Some of us make a mistake based on bad information, poor research, lack of experience, just plain laziness or any number of other factors. When a mistake on the job is made and the time comes to analyze why that mistake occurred, it's self-judgment time. This is the time to try to come to terms with how the decision was made and what the thought process was that led up to the decision. A person who is truthful with himself will not automatically just make an excuse for the mistake. Excuses are easy to come by. Sometimes the truth is not.

There is a difference between self-analysis and self-criticism. Criticism is fault-finding. Analysis is an examination or an investigation. A good executive must carefully balance these two. Many decisions are made within a business day. Some decisions must be made quickly while others can be given more time. We often have to make a quick decision based on the information we have at the time. Sometimes these quick decisions may be the wrong ones. It's okay to acknowledge a mistake or a poor judgment call. But, a more positive approach than kicking yourself over and over again for making a mistake is to examine the reasons why you made the mistake and prevent it from happening again. The danger of self-criticism is becoming paralyzed by the fear of making another mistake. Constantly second-guessing the decisions we've made can make us non-decisive or inactive.

As we analyze ourselves and our behavior, we have to find something about us or our job performance that we're proud of to balance our review of our mistakes.

Think About How to Improve

Healthy self-analysis brings personal improvement. It's important to try to look at yourself as others look at you, but it is very difficult to do.

One way to analyze yourself is to think about someone you admire. Think about the qualities that person has and list them. Then, try to think about your own qualities and list them. For example, is the person you admire friendly and personable? Think about your own personality. Are you shy? Do you have a hard time talking to other people? How does the other person approach people? Is she sincere? How can you learn from her?

Or think about a project you directed or worked on that you believe didn't go as smoothly as it should. What was your role in the project? Did people understand the directions you gave them? How could you have communicated better? Were you as organized as you should have been?

When asking yourself these questions, jot down your thoughts and solutions. Next time a similar situation arises, refer to your notes to make sure you've taken care of everything.

Improvement. Development. Growth. These are the rewards of positive self-analysis. With experience comes expertise. Improvement should be a constant goal in your daily life. How can you improve without growth and development? How can you face your family, your friends, your peers, associates and neighbors if you don't constantly search for ways to be better. Motivation must be a sincere inner driven force that's non-negotiable and a burning desire with you that is unrelentless. It must over power the complacency and procrastination that arises within all of us. These normal obstacles, that we all have, can be overcome by our personal commitment to excel and improve ourselves.

The mirror is the best tool! Use it. Have one visible in your every turn. This is the reflection to use and a reminder of who you are, where you are, how far you've come, where you are going and how you are growing.

3
The Art of Communication

It takes two for successful communication. Communication is like acting because acting is also reacting. Communication is a two-way (and sometimes three and four-way) interaction. So, when I say communication is like acting, I'm being serious. As acting is an art form, so is communication. Not everyone does it the same, and not everyone does it well.

Good communication is listening, understanding and perceiving a statement or situation. Good communication is based on full knowledge and comprehension of what you have discussed and heard.

Many times you can't verbally say something and expect it to be understood and received in exactly the same way you said it. There are many phrases that you can say several different ways and with different voice inflections that will mean different things to different people. Therefore, when communicating verbally, we need immediate feedback.

In business, the work you are doing must tie in with everyone else's work. Everyone has to communicate with one another in order to know what is going on around them and to see the entire picture. Key components of successful communication within a business include <u>verbalization</u>, <u>repetition</u>, <u>documentation</u>, <u>openness</u> and <u>correction</u>.

Could You Repeat That, Please?

One of the most common forms of communication is verbalization. We communicate with someone by talking to them; sharing information with them. Keep in mind, however, that individuals retain only about 17% of what they hear. This is one reason I believe that not only must employees have good training to do their jobs well, they must also be periodically retrained in the same jobs. If the person you're talking to only remembers about 17% of what you told them, that leaves 83% of what they heard up for open interpretation.

Therefore, repetition plays a key role in keeping communication lines open. In training someone <u>to do a job, it's necessary to go over and over and over the proper steps to make sure they understand.</u>

We have a procedure for making dough. It is a very simple procedure. I alphabetized it to make it even easier to understand. On a visit to one of our restaurants, I briefly told the employees during training, "You take A and you mix it with B and you add C and stir in D. Do you understand that?"

They replied, "Sure."

Well, that was my first mistake. Because, if I thought they were going to be stupid enough to admit that they didn't understand something that I had said so simply and make me think they were idiots, then I was being an idiot myself. No one was going to say, "No, I don't understand that."

But the truth of the matter is they didn't really understand it. When I physically got A and *mixed* it with B and *added* in

C and *stirred* in D, and then said, "Do you see that?" They said, "Yes!", and meant it.

So, I said, "Okay, now you do it." So they did. They took A, mixed it with B, added C and stirred in D, and they knew how to do make dough according to the procedure.

Well, that was fine. They had the procedure down; it was black and white and there was no problem. Time passed and because they are human beings, they became complacent. They went through the days and months and thought, "Gee, this is so simple. It's just A, B, C and D. I'll just throw all those in the bucket and stir it up. No problem, right?"

Surprise! All of a sudden, we found out the dough wasn't coming out the way it should. When the employees were questioned, they replied, "Don't know. We're doing it just the way you showed us!"

So, I got them together again, and I said, "You take A, mix it with B, add in C and stir in D." And I showed them again. And again. And again.

This story illustrates the real need for repetition. Retraining. It's important in communication to repeat our intentions or our company mission or our procedures and policies. Again. And again.

Repetition can also be a useful tool in *touchy* or *guarded discussions* and "arguments". If someone makes a statement that is <u>derogatory</u>, <u>angry</u> or <u>false</u>, instead of becoming angry or disgusted yourself, the best thing to do to control that communication is to calmly repeat back to them what they said and ask them if that is what they meant. If we're having an argument or difference of opinion, and I ask you to repeat something you said that sounded particularly irritating, if you repeat it, it will probably sound irritating to you as well. Always repeat what you heard, repeat it out loud so you all hear it. Then ask them if that is what they said. See what happens when you do! It's an effective way to gain control of a discussion or difference of opinion. This tool works well and can help you keep control of a potentially heated communication.

Write It Down

My mother was a great communicator. She laid out her expectations without a written handbook. I don't know how she did it. I've never been as good at it, but she certainly had her way of letting us know what she expected. She communicated with us in a way we could understand. She demanded honesty, hard work, attention to schoolwork and discipline. Her children were her life. We did as we were expected. Her willpower was enormous. One of her greatest fears was losing a child while she was alive. So, when her oldest child, my brother, was very ill and in failing health, she died first. I'm convinced that she willed it that way.

In the business world, most executives do not possess the ability to provide this level of communication. Therefore, written communication is viable, imperative and non-negotiable. It's the safest way to make certain that a verbal communication is truly understood by both parties. Putting your agreement in writing is the best way to avoid misunderstanding, especially in business. There are other forms of written communication that are equally important in business.

Policy and procedures handbooks, for example, are critical to a company's long range goals and planning processes. Procedures specifically lay out what is expected and demanded. A written procedure dictates the exact steps to be followed to get the exact results you expect. Policy handbooks need to be continually updated and upgraded. A policy statement can't be static. I value policy and procedure handbooks the same as long range planning. Anyone who doesn't look into the future doesn't have vision. It's important to revise policies and procedures every year because in business, as I keep saying, nothing stays the same, everything changes.

Keep Lines of Communication Open

Many people fail to get input and knowledge from others because they aren't willing to listen. You can learn from anyone. A close associate once pointed out to me the advantage of living in a small community is you come in contact with people from a variety of social spheres. In a large city, you have a tendency to associate only with your peers or the people in your neighborhood.

Referring to me, for instance, he said that I have friends that vary from hourly laborers to top executives to some of the most influential people in the world. I hadn't thought about it until he mentioned it. Now I realize how I benefit from knowing and learning from these many different types of people.

My dad never made more than $75 a week. But, he had more common sense than anyone I've ever known. As my career blossomed, and I had major decisions to make, I would often talk to him about them. Sometimes he didn't understand the technicalities of a situation, but he was never without an idea. He gave me a different perspective on things.

You never know who will give you a good idea. You can learn from the custodian in the building, the supplier, or the shipping and receiving people, if you're willing to listen and learn.

When someone shares an idea with me, I listen as if I've never heard it before. Then I say, "That's a great idea!" Even if I've heard it a dozen times before. At a meeting sometime ago, an individual that I thought had some adverse attitudes toward me came up and we started talking. I found out he didn't feel adversely at all. We got into a discussion about various business philosophies, and he said, "Plan your work, work your plan." Now, this was one of the first things I learned in business some 35 years ago. Those words had been repeated to me hundreds of times. But, it didn't hurt me to hear them again.

"That's great, that's really great," I said. He beamed with pride and continued talking about some interesting and very original ideas; ones I hadn't heard or thought about before. If I had told him "Yes, I've heard that," our conversation might have ended there and I would not have benefited from his other knowledge. Why should I stifle any kind of input? I appreciate the fact that someone is trying to help me. Many people get caught up in trying to show how smart they are and saying, "I know that."

There are times I would rather appear naive, because then people are going to tell me things which they otherwise might not. It's amazing how people will respond to you if you act like you don't know anything. People are more willing to share their ideas. It opens up the lines of communication. I have gained a favorable position in many negotiating or adversarial situations because I didn't tell anything that I knew and I acknowledged appreciation for everything that I was told in return. I like to work or negotiate in an arena where people think they're smarter or more knowledgeable than I am. Many times you can gain an advantage by appearing ignorant, stupid or dumb and thereby enhance your ability to control the outcome of the negotiations. However, you must possess the business acumen to know when to use this ploy and when it is important to show you understand and know what you're talking about.

When I was in the insurance business we used to have to get referred leads. One of the things I was taught to ask people was, "Could you give me an idea of someone who has just been promoted or has received a pay increase and might be interested in insurance?"

When my client would say, "Yes, John Brown," I didn't reply, "Oh yes, I know him." If I had the client may not have offered any other names, thinking I knew everyone they knew. Instead, I would smile and say, "Thank you," and usually, by keeping the communication lines open, I would get one or two other names as well.

Most people want to help you, if you'll just ask. Most people want to feel they're helping others. So why not capitalize on it? That desire to help can make your job a lot easier.

In our system, we make sure that the number of direct reports to each individual is controlled to a number that allows time to communicate without stress or pressure. We encourage programs that reward suggestions and new ideas or "old ones" that improve efficiency and eliminate costs and expenses. We give awards of trips, money, plaques and trophies for suggestions or ideas which will increase performance levels.

We have friendly competition among peers. New employees, in their indoctrination and training, are taught to share information. We have follow-up programs with checklists and procedures to follow.

These policies are executed at store manager level and supervised by our area general managers, who are supervised by district managers, who are supervised by regional vice-presidents, who report directly to our Executive Vice-President and our Chief Operating Officer.

Information is filtered on the way up, down and across, but never passed along or restrained without three opinions agreeing, with the exception of distribution directives. The basis of free input and majority rule is that no one is intimidated about making their opinions known.

In our inspection and observation reports from all levels, there is a request for input and analysis of progress and growth of our personnel. Our promotion policy is to try to promote from within. We try to have every position filled with an employee that is promotable. Every person working with a potentially promotable employee must be "pulling for that promotable" to get the job. Each employee working with that person must believe he or she is the right person for the job. It is my belief that unless you have the respect and admiration of everyone around you and all of them are supportive and want you to be promoted, including subordinates and superiors, you probably need to reassess yourself.

Correction Comes Through Re-Training

Whether you're a business owner, a manager or a supervisor, the time will always come when you have to help someone correct his or her behavior or work skills. I don't know anyone who enjoys having to reprimand an employee. Just the concept of reprimanding or criticizing someone brings on a negative connotation, and too often such situations can become negative. That's why I try to look at these situations as another "correction opportunity. "Criticism should always be constructive and not personal.

When I find myself in the situation of having to correct an employee, I first talk to them about how he or she has contributed to our company. I try to talk about situations in which the employee has done a good job. I try to start the discussion on a positive note. Then, I bring up the problem. I state very succinctly what I believe the problem to be and why I think it needs correction.

Here is a typical scenario. Let's say there is an employee in data processing or order processing whose work has become sloppy. I might start by saying, "Jane, thank you for putting in those extra hours last month to get that rush order out for us. Your effort really helped us make delivery on time."

Then I would get to the correction opportunity. "But, in the last two weeks, Jane, I've noticed your orders seem to have become sloppy. Twice your mistakes have caused us to miss a shipment and that just can't happen. Do you have any thoughts on why you've been making so many mistakes lately?" I then give the employee an opportunity to explain his or her side of the story. Together we agree on steps to take corrective action and make plans to meet later and evaluate the situation. I thank the employee again for her contribution to the company and try to mention something else she's done that is positive.

Perhaps Jane just needed to be reminded of the proper procedures for processing orders. Perhaps there were personal problems that were affecting her work; a sick child or spouse. Perhaps, as in the A,B,C & D example, she just got complacent about her work or decided to improvise on her own to save steps. She may need some retraining. It is better to cultivate and correct an existing employee than to lose the investment you have in that person and have to start all over again with a new employee. That becomes expensive. Hopefully you have developed effective lines of communication and the respect of your employees so that you can work through a few rough times and difficult circumstances.

One way to keep on top of problems, as I've mentioned before, is constant training and retraining of our employees. If employees are reminded on a regular basis about their job responsibilities, it helps keep problems from occurring.

<u>Again, communication. And repetition</u>. This takes the patience and effort to continually go back into retraining and review. The psychology is touchy! You may appear to think they are stupid when you cover something they have learned before. They may resent your "meddling." You have to cover this in advance through policy and procedures. Lay it out as part of the job. Let them "teach" you in retraining, then if they are doing it right, you've accomplished your purpose. If they are wrong you correct it simply and without fanfare. "Oh, I might point this out to you. It's easier to do it this way (which is the right procedure that worked so well they quit using it) right?"

4
Wanted - A Good Listener

If I walked up to you at a business meeting or social gathering, and you had never seen me before, I would introduce myself.

"Hi, my name is Gene Bicknell."

"My name is Tom Box," you would probably respond, and we would start a conversation. At the end of the conversation, I'd walk off in another direction and you probably wouldn't remember my name.

Has this happened to you? Have you ever wondered why? The reason is that while I was in the process of introducing myself, you most likely weren't listening. You were thinking about your own name, how to introduce yourself, or what you would say after telling me your name. So, you didn't catch my name.

The same thing happens, all too frequently, when we are in discussions. Instead of listening to the person who is talking, we're thinking about our next statement or rebuttal. We have a tendency to think that what we have to say is more important than what anyone else has to say.

You Can't Hear a Thing With Your Mouth Open

Have you ever noticed that God gave us two ears and only one mouth? Do you suppose he intended us to use our ears twice as much as our mouth?

We once had an executive who had more talent than many people I've known. Unfortunately, he didn't know how to listen. He talked constantly and when he was finished, although we knew everything he knew, he knew nothing that we knew.

I watched him one day when we were visiting a construction site. We arrived at the site together and walked into the construction trailer. He spread the plans out on a table and started talking. He kept talking for 45 minutes! No one else said a word. In fact, no one was able to get a word in! He talked non-stop to everyone working there; the contractors, the plumbers and electricians. He told them how he wanted things done but never once asked the opinion of anyone else. When he was through, he folded up the plans and walked out the door. There was no time for the workers to share their ideas or concerns. No opportunity to provide him with what would have been valuable input. The construction people were more knowledgeable than he was, but this ego-driven executive learned nothing from them. He was way off base and as a result missed some key concerns. Luckily, the construction workers solved the problems on their own, no thanks to the executive. And, by the way, he wasn't with us 90 days later!

None of Us Has All The Answers

At the age of 22, I became a supervisor at a Goodyear Tire Company plant. Most of the people on my crew had been at their jobs for 15 to 20 years. My first day on the job, I told them, "Look, I'm never going to know as much about this operation as you do." They were all skilled; they had the background and the experience that I lacked.

"The only way we will be successful," I told them, "is by you helping me to learn." I let them know that I would do my best to assist them in any way that I could, but that we would have to work together. By respecting their knowledge and ability, I encouraged them to share with me. By listening to them, I kept myself open to learn from them. As a result, our productivity levels were very high and we were chosen for many of the company's experimental runs.

The more you communicate, listen and ask for help, the more help you're going to get. Many people fail because <u>they think they</u> should have all the answers and make all the decisions. They don't want to ask for help or get input from others because they think it's a sign of weakness. They also mistakenly believe that by listening to others and sharing they compromise their "control."

The best executives, supervisors and workers are the ones who are willing to ask for help and then listen to suggestions that are given to them.

The ego says, "Listen to me. I am smart. I have all the answers." But to have good working relationships we have to control this voice. We have to be willing to accept and express the idea that none of us has all the answers.

When you're in business, you depend on other people to work hard for you and give you their honest input. If there's a problem, the opinions and suggestions of others just might result in a solution. To understand what you're dealing with, you have to have all the input and guidance you can get.

Listening Helps Build the Team

If you opened an office and hung a sign outside your door which simply read "Listener," you'd have more business than you'd ever need. There just aren't enough listeners in the world. Many people crave to have someone listen to their problems or thoughts. They will pay good money to be heard.

Does that sound far fetched? There are people who are starving to find somebody who cares about what's going on in their lives. If you don't believe me, try listening to one of the talk radio programs some night.

One of my sons and I had a conversation several months ago. It was an excellent talk, probably one of the best we've had in a long time. Know why? He did all the talking, I just listened.

My daughter, Diney, once taught me another lesson about listening. She sent me a Father's Day card, one year, that had written all over the front, "Yes Father, Yes Father, Yes Father" about 25 times. I opened the card to find "Yes Father," written about ten more times. At the very bottom it read, "I'm glad we had this little talk." Although meant as a joke, that card made a lasting impression on me.

Why does it always seem that when it comes to dealing with children, many parents don't take time to listen to them? I think we find it hard to listen to children because, as adults, we know how irrational and unthinking they can be. Remember my prior commentary on all the freedoms and privileges they want but aren't really ready to handle? Aside from those typical human behavior patterns, it's important to remember that children are adults who lack the experience, background and education that adults have. Even though we can't let children make decisions they shouldn't be making, it's important to let them know that we're listening to what they are saying. We may not agree with what they're saying, but they are entitled to their input.

Although they probably aren't aware of it, I have learned something from each of my children. They may be my son or daughter by chance but they are my friend by choice. That was on another plaque given to me by one of my children.

Gena taught me how to gain friends from honesty and kindness.

Mitch is the sweetest man I've ever known. He taught me how to be humble and let the "last word" come from the other person rather than let an argument develop.

Mike made me realize that having too much natural talent without knowing what you want to do with it will leave you unsettled and restless. Until you find your direction, superior intelligence can cause stress and duress. Once focused, that energy can conquer all.

Marty taught me the value of stability. Once he reached the maturity of adulthood, he has shown me how pleasant life can be if you live it right.

By listening and watching we learn. Listening to our children or a subordinate requires full knowledge that the power of being able to keep your mouth shut, even when you're a role model, is still an opportunity to learn.

It's Not Enough To Tell Someone You're Listening to Them

If you call on others to help you, for instance, in a <u>decision making process</u>, record on paper all comments that are made by everyone, so you don't forget and-most importantly-so the speakers know they are being taken seriously. Then, you must follow through. If a speaker gave input that helped seal the decision, <u>let that person know</u>. On the other side, if you didn't take the advice of those who gave input, be prepared to lay out and make accountable the reasons why you went the other way. Nothing is more frustrating to an associate than to perceive he or she isn't being listened to, especially if you ask for their advice. As the leader of your company, you must make your employees feel comfortable in expressing themselves and let them know their opinions and their input have value far beyond the most immediate decision or crisis.

Silence Can Help You Get More Information

The trick to listening is learning to turn your ears on and your mouth off. It's hard to do, especially if you have an opinion or statement that is just bursting to get out! The next time this happens to you, try keeping your lips sealed. Keep silent. Let the other person keep talking. This is a real test! The silence is mind shattering. You think you need to say something, but <u>don't</u>. A minute will seem like an hour. Don't give in and be the first one to speak. Wait it out and you will be pleased with the results.

Silence is uncomfortable for people, and that's another reason it's hard for us to keep quiet. Let's say you have a concern about a particular employee and you've gathered enough facts and information to visit with him or her about your concerns. Try not to do most of the talking.

After you've expressed your concerns, let him or her explain the situation. Don't interrupt. Don't make judgment statements. If she doesn't come forth with much of an explanation, let there be a moment or two of silence. The silence will be uncomfortable for both of you. Someone will be compelled to fill the dead air. Let it be the employee. Perhaps he or she will come forth a little more and give further explanation for their behavior. Listen to what they have to say. Ask questions, but try not to give your opinion about why he or she is doing this or that. Let him or her provide the information and then take the information and do what is best for your company.

You Have to Really Care

If you are not a good listener now, it's not too late. You can become a good listener if you are a sincere person. Many busy executives and business people are constantly on the move. Their minds are whirring all the time. Because they have so much to do, they take shortcuts. They feel they don't have the time or luxury of exploring all the input and listening to others.

To truly listen to people, you have to care about what they say. If you want your business to succeed, you MUST care about your employees and your customers.

If you are afraid or resent hearing negative feedback then you will not get factual information. Those involved in the discussion will recognize your attitude and they'll guard their comments. This is especially true if you are their supervisor or someone further up the management ladder.

Most people want to protect their own welfare and they are not going to be stupid enough to irritate their boss. They may not even want to irritate their peers.

As you perfect your listening skills you will notice that what people hear will often be taken out of context. **People hear what they want to hear.** Conveniently or untruthfully, they will claim you said something differently than what you actually said. Be sure you hear and perceive what is being said.

To illustrate this point, let me share a story my friend Jimmie Rodgers told me: A duck walks into a jewelry store and asks the proprietor, "Got any duck food?" He responds, "This is a jewelry store, we don't sell duck food in here, we sell jewelry."

The duck leaves, but comes back the next day, walks in and says, "Got any duck food?" The proprietor is agitated and says, " You're the same duck that came in here yesterday! I told you then, we don't sell duck food and we still don't! Now get out of here."

The third day the duck comes in again, "Got any duck food?" The jeweler is exasperated. "Listen, you've been in here three days in a row asking for duck food! You come in here one more time and ask that and I'm going to nail your webbed foot to the floor!!!"

The fourth day the duck comes in again. The jeweler is shocked. "Got any nails?" Dumbfounded, the jeweler responds, "This is a jewelry store, we don't sell nails."

The duck responds, "Got any duck food?"...

Listening is a skill, and an art, but also a trait that must be developed. Sincerity is its strongest component! You have to want to be a good listener!

1. Can I repeat what I heard? *(Do it!)*
2. Did I understand the meaning of what was said? *(Ask!)*
3. Do they believe what they said? *(Read their eyes and voice)*
4. How strong are their convictions relative to their statements?
5. How do I really, truthfully, feel about their statements?

When you practice your listening skills, be forewarned that you will not succeed in becoming a good listener if you are insincere about it. Listening is a people skill. You've got to genuinely care about people and like them because listening is part of caring about people.

Most people skills are difficult to develop for individuals who don't really like people. Take the challenge each day or at least each week, to learn all you can about someone you have contact with on a regular basis. Ask them questions about their life, their rearing, their decisions in life's choices. Listen and remember. Ask about their family, their childhood dreams, their education, their hobbies. Listen for tragedy, accomplishments, experiences. Ask if there is one thing that changed their life. Ask why they chose their occupation and education.

Do this over and over with different people. You'll be amazed at the response you receive from them and how much influence they'll have in your behalf to other individuals around them.

5
What you don't know CAN hurt you

As each person goes through a career track, they gain experience and knowledge that helps them along the way to eventually become experts in their field.

I know many people who are perfectly content to find a niche or a job in which they can operate comfortably and then stay there the rest of their working lives, unchallenged. That's okay for some people. But it's not okay for a person who intends to grow professionally and raise their level of income or expertise substantially. I don't know of any successful people who don't have an almost unquenchable thirst for knowledge and a desire to continually grow intellectually, professionally and socially.

When you think about it, gaining knowledge throughout your professional life is really quite easy. We gain knowledge in three ways: passively (receiving information from someone;) witnessing, (watching what happens to others in situations;) and experiencing, (learning as we go academically or self-professing).

The first way to gain knowledge is to receive information from a person or a source we trust is giving us good information. We listen to the information given to us, and we learn from it. It's passive learning, but it is still important.

This form of knowledge is exemplified in the parent-child relationship or a teacher-student relationship. It's one person of experience or authority handing down information to someone who doesn't have the same experience. Unfortunately, as most parents know, children don't always believe their parents have the intelligence or knowledge they say they have. And, some employees just don't believe their boss when he or she tells them the downside of an idea or concept. Just as parents seem to gain more knowledge as their children grow up, employers seem to gain knowledge as their employees make mistakes.

We can tell our children they shouldn't drive fast. We tell them they shouldn't use drugs or drink alcohol. Kids may listen to some of that advice, siphon out what they wish to abide by, and then you know what usually happens to the rest of that advice. That is why passive learning is important, but it's not the most important way we learn.

The second way to gain knowledge is by watching what happens to other people. If you see a friend or an acquaintance get arrested for drug use or driving under the influence or someone put in jail for theft, you realize immediately that you don't want that to happen to you. It's so easy to see the results when it happens to someone else. Often, we may find ourselves thanking our lucky stars that WE weren't caught doing what others have been caught doing. This may cause us to alter our behavior, so therefore, we've gained knowledge. However, gaining knowledge in this manner doesn't always have to focus on such negative things as arrests or mistakes other people make. We can learn from watching successful people as well.

There is such a wealth of information and resources that it is easy to "study up" on a certain individual or role model we might admire. While our news media seems to report on mostly negative things, there are many media and magazines that focus on the study of successful people or successful companies. It has always amazed me how many successful people are out there in the world who seem "just like me." They live in smaller communities; they began their businesses very conservatively and have followed conservative values in keeping their business successful. I follow the careers of successful business people like the Leprinos and the Athertons and learn from them.

A watchword called "mentoring" has been kicked around for several years now. It may seem cliché, but mentoring is very important in gaining knowledge. Mentoring is having the opportunity to be taken under someone's wing and guided along a path of learning. A mentor is much more than a teacher or an instructor. A mentor is more of a friend or close associate who truly cares about another individual's success. Those people who can find such a close associate are very lucky. They have a built-in resource for gaining all kinds of knowledge in business or professional areas.

The third, and probably most important, way of gaining knowledge is through experience. Nothing beats experience in business. We all learn as we go. Each day brings a lesson in life if we are alert and mindful of it.

It's like the young child who is told by the parent not to get to close to the flame on the stove because he might get burned. But the flame is so pretty and so alluring, and the child just has to reach out for it... When the burn occurs and the child is crying in pain, that's when the reality of the lesson really sinks in. The child most likely will not reach for the flame again.

So it is in business. Good business people and executives look at each decision or action they take and think about what went right, what went wrong and what needs to be changed. Every day brings a new experience and a new lesson to be learned.

Knowledge, as we visualize it, is so diversified. Knowledge has to be siphoned and sifted out, along with reality. We have to have an alert and open mind that will engulf every opportunity to learn. We have to have the ability to store that knowledge and pull it back up when we need to use it.

Again, refer to the statement, "It worked so well that I quit using it." Many times we have to be reminded of the things we already know so we can go out and start doing the right things again and use the good sense that we've accumulated throughout our experience.

We must take in all the information we can and learn from others and our own experiences as we guide our careers on the track we want them to take.

Knowledge is Power

Knowledge is contagious. The more you have the more you want. Knowledge can come from your own intellect, or it can come from other individuals. Holiday Inn founder Kemmons Wilson said it perfectly, "One pound of learning requires ten pounds of common sense to apply it."

Look around at the people you consider leaders or high achievers. I suspect you'll see that these people never seem to lose their desire to learn. They are intent on increasing their skills and knowledge. They don't stand still; are never static.

No one can know everything. That would be impossible. However, you can know where to find any information and you can let other people help you. It goes back to people skills. If you are a good communicator and a good listener, knowledge will come to you. Knowledge is freedom. We have the freedom and the right to acquire all the knowledge we want. Sometimes, we take that freedom for granted.

It's More Than Just Book Learnin'

Remember when you were a kid and you couldn't wait until the day you could get out of school? I do. I'd sometimes think to myself that if I could get finished with school, I'd know everything I needed to get on with my life.

That's the short-sighted view of an immature youngster. Of course, if we're smart, our education never ends, even when the "book learnin" stops.

While knowledge provides freedom, it also provides information, wisdom and enlightenment. Today's technological world provides us with all kinds of information we never dreamed we'd be able to access. There's so much information out there, it would be impossible to access it all. I know there is information out there that could help me run my business better and make more enlightened decisions. Some of that information will come to me naturally, through the daily process of business. Each experience provides me with additional information and knowledge. Each success and each *mistake* provide me with knowledge.

Other knowledge I have to take an active role in obtaining. Sometimes, I have to call a business associate or a friend for advice. Or, I have to go find reference materials to help me look for answers or understand a situation.

When you realize how much you really don't know, it can be humbling. It doesn't matter how successful you are, every business venture has some kind of risk and some type of learning curve.

Many companies are venturing into international development. We are no exception. I was instrumental in developing the first Pizza Hut outside the continental United States. The development was in Vancouver, Canada. A Canadian partner was necessary, as Canadian laws and restrictions on imports became an obstacle we needed to overcome. We chose our real estate agent in Vancouver. That experience has helped me learn a great deal about business outside our country. Subsequently there have been many other experiences with many other countries around the world that have built on that knowledge.

We learned habits, practices and lifestyles and how they affect the way other countries do business. You can't force United States business practices on other cultures. You have to learn the other country's business customs and practices and treat those practices and customs with respect. That's the one universal law that applies in international business-treat individuals and their customs with respect!

Common courtesy and kindness are applicable in all countries. Cordiality, friendliness, positive attitudes and compliments go a long way. Open-mindedness and a riddance of preconceived ideas will open your mind to a lot of new and exciting experiences if you're only willing to learn.

The new buzz word these days is "paradigm shift". A paradigm is a preconceived method of operation. Simply put, it's the "way it's always been done" syndrome. When you shift away from an established paradigm, you open your mind to doing things a completely different way. You explore the possibilities, whether or not they are realistic.

Our changing world and changing cultures are causing all of us to shift our paradigms. The "way we've always done things" quite possibly won't work in the future. People who are open to gaining knowledge are open to exploring possibilities and opportunities from which others close themselves off.

Watch out for people who say, "No problem", the most universally used phrase in global business. Many citizens of different cultures will agree with you and then drag their feet or never do as they have said they would.

First-Hand Experience is Best

As I stated earlier, I was amazed at the amount of intelligence my parents gained from the time I was 16 until I was 21. For some reason, at about 21 I realized that they had information and know-how that I could learn from. From the time I was in my mid-20's until their deaths, I was always interested in and sought their opinions and viewpoints on just about everything I did. I didn't always use their advice, but they always gave me a different perspective.

When I was 18 and looked at my parents I saw limited knowledge. Then at 21, I looked at them again and I was amazed at how much they had learned. In three years they had become so knowledgeable that I wondered how they did it in only three years. What happened to me between the ages of 18 (when I knew everything) and 21 (when I realized how little I knew)? Experience! Witnessing.

You'll learn more from first hand experience than you will by reading a textbook or listening to someone. This is academic learning versus real world experience. By getting your feet wet and plunging in the middle of something, you're forced to confront it. You'll gain knowledge quickly. It's kind of like finding out how tough someone is when you get into a fist fight with them. Incidentally, when getting in a fist fight you should always smile, that way when they hit you, it breaks only one lip.

In a business situation, active training programs provide that first-hand experience to your potential and current employees. It's not enough to send them a memo or give them a policy handbook when they walk in your door. Employees have to be shown how to do the job they're going to be expected to do. They have to be trained how to read and interpret an order. They have to be shown the steps necessary to enter an order and then they have to sit down and enter the order themselves.

It's back to the A,B,C & D process again. You can tell them and you can show them but until they sit down at the computer with their notes and their knowledge and enter their first few orders they won't really understand. And, there'll be mistakes.

Why?

Because they haven't done the process enough to really know what they're doing. They will gain knowledge about their job only by doing it. And the more they practice, the more they do the actual work, the better they will be.

The training process takes time. Often it will take weeks or even months. That's why it's so important to periodically retrain employees. Having good, long-term, well-trained employees helps a company run smoothly. Frequent turn-over and constant training of new people is a drain on a company and an indication that something is very wrong with the operation. Depending on the technicality of your operation, it can take six months to a year for an employee to become a profitable investment in your company. Training is a high cost in time and money when you run a business. But, training is essential. The job can't be done without it. The employees can't do their jobs without the knowledge they gain from training.

Retraining is even more important. Retraining supports the base of our knowledge. The most important employees you have are the ones who know their job and are doing it well. Training is essential. Retraining is imperative!

Look At All The Angles

My favorite poet is T. S. Eliot. He is a poet of depth and magnitude. I can read one of his poems and find four or five different meanings within the framework of his writing.

Years ago, during a discussion with another individual about philosophy, attitudes and opinions, he asked, "Have you ever read Georgier, a 14th century Russian philosopher?"

I hadn't, so he said, "Wait here." He left, went to a book store, bought the book and brought it back to me. It was an 80 page book, in hardback cover, and I thought, " Great, 80 pages, I can read this in about 30 or 40 minutes."

Wrong!

I read the first page and I thought. I read the second page, then went back and read the first page again. I read the third page and then the first two again. *Every time I read it, I found a different opportunity for thought.*

That's what a true philosopher accomplishes. That's what we try to accomplish in our business scheme. You have to look at all angles and try to envision all the possibilities. We try to establish a philosophical and conservative approach to how we do business so it will attract feedback. People will come up with ideas and new ways of looking at things and this provides learning opportunities for all of us. There is so much untapped knowledge among our employees and associates that we fail to expose because we can't concentrate on obtaining it or encouraging participation. Sharing knowledge is stimulating at all levels.

Keep Yourself Organized

With a few exceptions, most busy executives became busy executives because they took pains to work hard and learn more about what they were doing. Most busy executives I know are motivated to continue to gain knowledge. It's an essential quality. If an executive is too busy to learn, he won't be an executive for long. To keep seeking knowledge, it's important to have a sense of organization about your job and your life. Time has to be set aside for learning.

It comes down to planning, preparing and scheduling. If you're organized, regardless of how busy you are, you can find a half hour or an hour to read a motivational book. (Try the Bible. It's one of the most motivational books I know.) Prepare notes or questions you need to ask for your meeting tomorrow. Jot down ideas. Prepare. Take a few moments to analyze what happened in your day and think about what you did right or what you did wrong. How could you better handle a similar situation in the future? This is gaining knowledge. It sounds simple and it is. But it's a freedom too often neglected or taken for granted. Think about it this way...if God has given you a perfectly working body, why would you abuse it with drugs, alcohol or other irresponsible behavior? If you have common sense, you won't. God gave human beings a mind and a thirst for knowledge and adventure. Why not take advantage of this great gift? Use it. Don't waste it.

Read of the great adventures where the examples are good and bad. People who have used their God-given talents in good ways and those who have abused them. Dictators who have forced their wills and selfishness on the weak and unsuspecting. Kings who cared and those who didn't. The carelessness and deceit of rulers against their people. Jesus only taught love and forgiveness and he was crucified for it. Many who love or care are often condemned as well. Some of the most generous and caring people are often the most criticized and chastised of all. Those who benefit from the generosity and kindness of these individuals are the first to find fault.

Society and Disregard for Life and Rules (Laws)

We are creating a society (at least part of it) of non-caring, irresponsible, unaccountable attitudes and approaches to everything in life. From turning our backs on innocent people being beaten and robbed or raped, and ignoring cries for help because we don't want to "get involved."

Being late for meetings or work days or not showing up when you're supposed to is rude, inconsiderate and irresponsible. People need structure in their life to be productive and efficient. If unstructured persons mix with structured persons it usually causes conflict and disruption.

Now we get into what's your priority. What do you want to be? What's important to you? Do you want to be considerate, effective and accountable, or do you just not care about anyone else? Are you selfish, self-centered, eccentric, egotistic or unconcerned about anyone else? If so, anything you hear or read will not change you.

We are here to tell you how to improve yourself because it gets you further in life, happier and satisfied. You may wonder sometimes when you do good things if it's worth it, if it's appreciated and why you're wasting your time (you're not!), but it will work to your advantage in the long run. Believe me, people who care and do caring things are going to be pleased and rewarded in the long run.

Don't do good deeds expecting rewards or appreciation. Only do them from your heart for the love of fellow human beings.

Gaining knowledge is a lifetime objective. You simply can't stop learning. Do good things and deeds. It will make you feel good about yourself and that is the greatest reward of all.

Recognizing others' knowledge and the resourcefulness thereof is a trait we should also develop. If we fail to give credit or recognize the wisdom of our associates, peers, or superiors we could make a major mistake.

One of my associates, a person I promoted to a top position, made the mistake of telling another associate that I didn't understand the business. I would not tell that person that I know he made that statement because it would serve no purpose.

Why would a person make a statement like that? Most likely to improve their personal status by indicating they have more knowledge than the person they are speaking about. It may be to discredit their superior and make themselves look better. It may be to impress an associate. It may be to prove a point. The reason doesn't really matter, the point is you leave yourself vulnerable when you say something negative that you can't substantiate. Don't let your mouth overload your brain. There is nothing to be gained by making a derogatory statement. Remember the old adage, "If you can't say something nice, don't say anything at all."

Set an example for your children and instill in them the importance of treating their fellow students with respect, friendliness and kindness. Encouraging them to treat everyone as an equal and to include everyone in all activities will get them established in proper behavior and learning patterns and teach them the importance of developing good relationships with everyone.

You never know when someone with whom you've had contact before will be a key player in a future situation. Treating someone nicely may be helpful to you later on. Even if that never happens, it leaves a good feeling and impression of you when you show respect to people. The impression we leave with those who intersect our life will remain long after we have continued through the intersection. Why do anything that isn't courteous or kind? It just isn't smart. Having positive relationships with people always makes me feel good.

6
Ego-Beware of Empire Building

1. There is no limit to what you can achieve or accomplish, if you don't care who gets the credit.
2. Working as a team is the key to success.

Unfortunately, when the individual ego demands attention, it is often the leader of a team who prevents teamwork.

The ego is the enemy of teamwork. The ego says, "Look at me. See what I've done. Isn't it great?"

Of course, the ego can be a motivating force, but left unchecked, it can ruin a team. For an organization to achieve success, all members must work toward the same goal. The ego only works for itself.

The favorite saying of a football coach I know is, "There is no 'I' in the word 'team'." As coaches (CEOs, managers, supervisor), we must work at removing the "I" in our own teams and in our behavior. We must put our egos aside and work for the team.

Keeping Egos Under Control

Ego is a great motivator. Ego itself, is a driver, a stimulant and we all have egos. The challenge is to not let ego override common sense. We have to be able to decipher and weed out the factors we want to keep and those we don't need.

If our ego dominates our personality, dominates the conversation in a group, or it fails to listen, then we lose many important opportunities. The ego becomes visible and people recognize it.

There's something about an ego that gets in the way of good relationships. If you want to see egos at their most effective and destructive, look at athletes. Many superstar athletes are normally very nice people. Even though they have an ego, they still treat everyone the way they would like to be treated. However, there are some excellent athletes who never make it to the professional level because they get too wrapped up in their egos. One of the complaints about sports today is there are too many superstars and not enough super teams. Elevating certain athletes to a level over their teammates can demoralize a team. After all, I don't know of many sports where one player can take the place of the entire team. One player can dominate but he still has to have the support of the rest of the team to be great. No matter how good the quarterback....without a receiver, he's nothing!

The compliment that means the most to me is when people tell me I'm no different now than when I had nothing. Another compliment I enjoy is that I treat everyone the same, regardless of social position or importance. I truly believe that each person, no matter what their financial or social status, deserves common courtesy and respect. I also believe in treating young people with respect. The mistake a lot of people make with youngsters is talking down to them. As I said earlier kids are just adults-in-waiting. They simply lack the experience and exposure that adults have had.

An ego is like a force. It's like an electrical current. It can be as effective at 110 volts as it can be at a thousand volts, depending on how it's utilized. Ego controls us if we allow it. We must control it. We must control the urge to say, "Look at me, aren't I great!"

As I said earlier, a person is much more impressive and powerful if her feats or accomplishments are stated and recognized by other individuals. If you've done something truly great or outstanding, it will be recognized or spoken of by another person. That's much more impressive. A third party's comments are strong! Our comments about ourselves can be bragging. Be sure you know the difference.

The Bigger a Person's Head Gets, the Easier it is to Fill Their Shoes

I can't stand arrogant people. I don't believe any person, no matter how successful, or rich, or powerful they are, should give off an air of arrogance. It's a complete turn off. But more than that, arrogance can be detrimental to a business.

A recent example of how arrogance by a U.S. Navy captain almost caused a disaster is evident in the following story.

A radio transmission released by the Chief of Naval Operations in October 1995 reads like this:

Station #1: Please divert your course 15 degrees to the North to avoid a collision.

Station #2: Recommend you divert YOUR course 15 degrees to south to avoid a collision.

Station #1: This is the Captain of a U.S. Navy ship. I say again, divert YOUR course.

Station #2: No, I say again, you divert YOUR course.

Station #1: THIS IS THE AIRCRAFT CARRIER ENTERPRISE.
WE ARE A LARGE WARSHIP OF THE U.S. NAVY.
DIVERT YOUR COURSE NOW!
Station #2: This is the Puget Sound lighthouse. It's
your call.

The higher you think you are on the totem pole, the harder you fall when you slip off the top. Egos are like balloons. One tiny pin prick can destroy the whole structure.

Share The Workload...Share The Credit

As I said earlier, it's hard to predict how a person will handle power. When you take an employee who has been with your company for a number of years and has been a great contributor and promote him to a supervisory or management position, how will he handle it?

Some new managers take on their added responsibility with vigor and are eager to be leaders of their team. They know their co-workers and have their respect (or they wouldn't have been promoted). They treat their co-workers with respect and encourage participation, communication and teamwork.

But some new managers have trouble with the added responsibility and power. They see their promotion as license to "get even" with some of their co-workers or former supervisors. They wreak havoc on the team and become quite skilled at covering their own hides. This kind of manager takes credit for all the accomplishments of his team; thus destroying the morale of his co-workers.

When I introduce or talk about an employee, I make it a point to say that employee works "with" me, not "for" me. I believe this is the proper attitude for a boss or manager to have. Yes, employees report to a manager and work under the direction of a manager. However, good managers and executives know that their recognition of a job well done will come only if their team supports them and does a good job.

Remember, people work "for" a lot of things. They work for money, for self-improvement, for self-satisfaction. They work for their families, subsistence, gratification of a temporary desire or material things. All of these are the things people work "for", not YOU!

Recently, I was honored by having my name placed on the Wall of Fame at Baxter Springs Historical Societies Museum. Not only was I proud to receive such an honor from my "roots" but many friends and relatives that I have known over the years attended the event. Phyllis Abbot, Mayor Wayne Cook, Bud Johnson, Mary Byrd (a former employer) all said a few words and then I was presented a plaque to commemorate the recognition. My picture will hang with Hale Irwin, Joe McCartney, Hubert Bird, Glad Robinson Youse and Dean Sims.

I have had the good fortune to receive many honors. I have been inducted into three Halls of Fame, and honored at a film festival. This particular recognition meant a great deal to me. The most meaningful thing is when these people who have known me and watched me over the years tell me I'm still the same person I was as a youth and poor.

I've talked before about working for Crocker's Bakery at age 11 and then Mrs. Crocker becoming my ward in her elder years. I've mentioned the three years at Read's Drug Store where I worked as a soda jerk. Then there was Karbe's grocery store, with two of my brothers, working for Ted Edens. Hard work. I can't forget Byrd's Drive-In, as first a soda-jerk and then a fry cook. After that it was back to Karbe's and then on to college. I was earning my own keep, paying my school expenses, buying my own clothes, autos and making my own spending money. All of this was child-labor as we know it today!

Was it a bad thing? I don't think so. If I couldn't have worked, I would have been frustrated and had no way to provide for myself. My parents couldn't help me. What direction would my life have taken if I couldn't have earned the money to provide me with my needs?

I often wonder if we are making a mistake by *not making* it possible for our youth to work. Most of them don't want to work. I didn't either. I had no choice. It took me two years to get my first full time job. I started at nine. It was my independence! My individualism! As a shy youngster and ashamed of my surroundings, I needed the self-confidence that earning my own keep instilled in me.

If our penal system provided jobs for offenders, especially juveniles, their chances for rehabilitation would be better, I think. We release them back into the same environment with no opportunities. Give them a chance to work. Require them to work. <u>Busy people</u> are happy people!

PART III

DEVELOPING OUR SKILLS

1
Exploring Our Ambitions

What do you expect of this life? From yourself? From anyone? Are you optimistic or pessimistic? Are you a realist? Only you can determine what you want to do; what you become; where and how far you go. It all depends on how much you want it; how much effort you are willing to put into your dream.

Your challenge is to determine, in your lifetime, how you want to fit into the overall scheme of things. Our country is a democracy. You have the personal freedom and ability to be creative. You can drive yourself beyond your own limitations, you can reach down and find the attitude that you can and will succeed.

Despite all our political problems, what makes this country great is that the little guy can make it big. That attitude has held this country together and it is an attitude that other, more historical countries are turning to every day.

Some of our forefathers came from Europe, where you were either born into royalty, wealth or poverty. Those same individuals who came to this country, primarily for freedom, lived through the entrepreneurial spirit, through capitalistic attitudes, through the opportunity to find work and earn a living in a positive environment.

Communism has been a relatively short lived form of government. It is dying because there is no incentive to be ambitious. There is no reason to work harder because your destiny is already determined. Hard work and commitment go unrewarded. Ambition is stifled.

In America, even the poorest of souls can go beyond where they originated, if they have the right attitude and determination. When I was very young, I was ashamed to have anyone take me home because our house didn't have a good coat of paint. It was rental property and rather run down. It didn't look like the homes of the other kids. I always asked to be let out a block or so away hoping no one would see the house and realize we were poor.

When I was six or seven years old, I started looking for a job. I wanted to make some money so I would be able to do things for myself. I can remember asking retailers or other business people if they had any work I could do. Naturally, I was still too young, even in those days. I decided to plant a vegetable garden. When my harvest was ready, I went door to door selling my produce. Sometimes I cut lawns. As I said earlier, I got my first "real" job at eleven. It was a great feeling to have a few dollars in my pocket. I was very conservative with my money (still am). I wouldn't blow it on ice cream or other treats. I did enjoy an occasional movie, but I rarely bought candy, popcorn or a soda.

Even back then I had a certain attitude. Deep inside of me was a burning desire to be successful. I was always aware of my surroundings and who was doing what. I was so enamored by people who had their own businesses and people who had wealth. I was convinced that some day, some how, some way, I too would be in a position to have nice things. That burning desire created an entrepreneurial spirit that encouraged me to constantly look for ways to make the money I desired.

After college and the military, I went to work for Goodyear Rubber Company. Even though I was in a management position, any time there were extra hours offered to do a janitorial job or work an extra shift, I always took it. Many times I would work double, even triple shifts because it was an opportunity to make more money.

If making money is important...setting a portion of your money aside in savings is even more important. Having some extra money saved allows you to take advantage of opportunities that might make you even more money. Saving is an investment. Sometimes, it seems as if you just can't do it, especially if you are a young family trying to make ends meet. Keep in mind that saving is an investment; have an attitude about saving, no matter how small the amount. You will be surprised how quickly it can multiply and that "nest egg" might provide an opportunity for greater financial gain. Without a start, you never get to go! Never bet on a race unless you're in it.

Earlier generations were taught to save some of their earnings. They had to. There was no Social Security, no Medicare or Medicaid, no government programs to pick them up if they stumbled. If they were to have any security for their later years, they had to provide it for themselves. Most everyone planned accordingly. They would put 50 cents or $1 aside. They saved for 40 years for emergencies, unexpected expenses and their old age.

Then, inflation, cost of living increases, changes in monetary values happened. Suddenly their lifetime of planning goes sour.

They can't get by on their savings. They are forced to find supplemental employment in their senior years. Even today, with all the government programs, benefits and subsidies, many seniors are forced to supplement their income by working.

This whole scenario poses the question of whether our government has actually helped citizens be more self-sufficient or caused them to be more dependent on social programs.

I've never been envious of other people's successes. Even when I was extremely poor and had very little starting out, I was always happy when someone else was able to be successful or reach a high level of earnings. I knew that most people worked hard to achieve their goals. I knew that I, too, would someday attain that level of success. That faith kept the inner desire alive. I watched other successful people and learned from them. I became aware of what opportunity really is and how to take advantage of it.

Remember though, an opportunity is not an opportunity unless you are in a position to take advantage of it. If you don't have the money or the other resources to take advantage of it then, you don't have an opportunity at all, just some good financial data.

How Do We Accomplish Our Goals?

Be confident in the goals you set for yourself.

When I was in the life insurance business, I learned to evaluate individual responses. Commission selling is the toughest kind of occupation. If you aren't having a lot of luck, you wonder when the sales will come. If you are doing well, you worry about when the sales will stop. The yo-yo effect of worry and stress kept me constantly on edge.

Commission selling takes a lot of self-starting and motivation. The rejections and denials are difficult to accept. No matter how hard you try, you take the "no's" as a personal failure. Everyone wants what life insurance will buy in benefits, but nobody wants life insurance. The cost interferes with buying new cars, boats, furniture or appliances. As difficult as selling was, training new sales people was even harder. Getting trainees to be self-starters and make the necessary "cold-calls" is as difficult as anything I've ever done. The knowledge I gained and the lessons I learned have been invaluable. Those skills have helped me throughout my entire career. If the education had been for sale, I couldn't have afforded it and wouldn't have learned it so completely.

Self-confidence is a good asset to possess, but only if you can truly evaluate yourself and your abilities. If you feel you've been passed over for a promotion or a new assignment, take an honest careful inventory of yourself. Where do you differ from the person who was promoted? This is a difficult task because most of us don't want to own up to our shortcomings. But honest evaluations are a must for success. Ask your supervisor for help. Resolve to become so productive that they can't afford to pass you by again.

Do You Have a Plan to Reach Your Goals?

Setting goals is the easy part. Having a plan to reach the goal is harder. It might take money. It might take extra long hours or personal sacrifices. But...you must have a plan in place or your goal will be unattainable.

If you want to open your own business, you are going to have to build up capital. You can't get loans or money to start a business unless you have a plan, so you need a business plan. We'll talk about how to develop a business plan later in this book. Don't make the mistake of thinking you can get others to give you the capital based on your brilliant idea. Too many times the one with the brilliant idea, but no money of their own in the business, find themselves out the door when the other investors think they know how to run the business better.

Don't Give Up the First Time You Fail

Success is hard to come by. Everyone makes mistakes. Only a few are lucky enough to win the first time they try something. You have to lay the proper groundwork, but even that is no guarantee that your business will succeed. Economic factors might come into play that you hadn't considered. Other factors, like tax laws and new minimum wage laws might punch holes in your whole plan. You have to be flexible enough to perceive and react to change. A sense of intuition and urgency is vital.

Pursue an Attitude of Excellence

Attitude is **all** important. It's the most significant factor in motivating success. Very few of us have natural talents and gifts. Not many of us can be professional athletes or possess photographic memories. Most of us have to work hard to hone whatever innate talents or skills we possess.

Excellence only comes from hard work and determination. You must have the *desire* to be the BEST!! Remember the $5 job!

Everyone has to believe in something! Why not believe in yourself? Be a doer! Of course it's hard and takes commitment. It's hard to stay concentrated and focused. You must be relentless and unyielding in your desire to accomplish your goal. You will have to give yourself pep talks constantly. Resist the desire to give in or give up!

<u>Mental toughness</u> - is a subject all its own. You've got it or you can develop it. It's when a runner wants to give in and fall back, but he doesn't. It's when a boxer is beat up, on the canvas and losing a fight and wants to give up or "throw in the towel", but he or she doesn't. Sometimes they go on and win!

They fight the battle bold and when the challenge is over no one can say they didn't give their "all."

That is "mental toughness".

2
Improving Our Abilities

Do you know what your strengths are? If you had to sit down and make a list of your strengths and weaknesses, how would you go about it? Do you really know yourself?

Knowing yourself is the key to improving yourself. Throughout our lives, we gain experience and abilities. Most people have some kind of natural talent. Many people have several talents. Most of us have to work very hard at honing the talents we have. First, however, we have to identify what those talents are.

Once you have identified your talents, how do you go about improving them? Actually, there are lots of ways to improve our abilities. We can learn from books (academically). We can learn by repetition, or doing something over and over again, thereby improving with experience. We can follow an organized procedure or system laid out for us in a systematic manner. We can learn by memorizing the exact steps or formula.

For the most part, our abilities fall in two areas: One category is skills. What are the skills we possess? The second category is mental - our self-confidence and self-esteem.

Every team or business has a need for certain skills. People who have certain skills must be found, trained and placed in their appropriate positions with the team or business. Therefore, each of us must identify the skills we have to offer. For some professions, certain skills are a necessity. An architect has to have drawing, drafting, geographic and mathematical skills. An attorney must be able to write and speak clearly. A physician must have specific skills in his or her area of practice. A surgeon must have steady hands and nerves. Some people have skills that they may not even be aware of or deem important. Yet, these skills may be critical within the framework of a team or business.

We talk a lot about *people* skills, almost to the point of it being a cliché, but people skills are very important in a team environment. Remember, there is no "I" in the word "team." So, in order to function in a team environment, one must be able to communicate with their peers, be friendly and be receptive to ideas and critiques. The message here is to not only identify obvious skills that have been developed through academic or professional training but also identify skills gained through other experiences. For example, focus is a skill. Being able to pay attention to detail and catch little irregularities is a part of having focus.

We could go on and on about skills, but the point is to identify your strongest skills, your adequate skills and your weakest skills. Depending on where you want to work or what you want to achieve, you need to determine which skills need improving and find a way to improve those skills.

A quick and easy example of this need is computer training. Most businesses these days rely heavily on computers. Even the 50-year-old executive who has always had a secretary and never had to type a word in his life can benefit from some computer training. Why? Because he may have to make a decision about which computer system to install in his business. He may have to develop a new data entry flow system to keep the work moving quickly through the office. If he has never even sat down in front of a computer, how can he hope to make an intelligent decision or evaluation?

In business, if you see areas in which improving certain skills would improve your longevity or promotability with the company, you would be well advised to find a way to gain or improve those skills. I'm not advocating becoming something you are not or learning a job you don't enjoy. This is all about knowledge-gaining and improving yourself. A little knowledge and experience can go a long way. The trick is to know your limitations and expand on your areas of opportunity.

Happy is the person who can find and accept her place in life and be content to justify her existence based on what she is doing for her livelihood - molding her existence by being comfortable with herself and constantly making her skills better by perfecting her activity on a daily basis.

In addition to identifying and improving certain skills we need to evaluate and identify strengths and weaknesses in our own personalities. This is where the mental part comes in.

There are many talented people in the world who could accomplish many important things if they weren't so afraid of something. That something could be the fear of failure or maybe even success, fear of spending too much money, or fear of disapproval from friends or family. Fear has a tremendous impact on people. How many times have you heard yourself say or think, "I could never do that!"

There are certain things you should not do, and fear plays a part in keeping people from doing foolish or harmful things. However, many times, fear unnecessarily limits us in achieving our dreams and goals.

The ethical and emotional breakdown in business over the last 50 years has followed the similar course of the family breakdown. Moral obligation and commitment has become compromised and relinquished by procrastination and avoidance of trust and integrity.

I still believe that by loyal and truthful commitment to fairness and treating others the way you want to be treated is the best way to <u>maintain</u> success and receive gratification. Dignity to all, respect to all, equality to all and recognizing everyone as an equal. Never talk down or look down at anyone, even children. Listening with sincere interest to whatever the other person is saying and truly hearing them will reap rewards!

Some of us have certain traits and characteristics that make us appear less believable and sincere than we are. Learn your characteristics and mannerisms and how they come across to others. <u>Record your normal conversational voice and listen to yourself.</u> You may be amazed and shocked by what you hear yourself saying. It may sound different than you mean.

Written words and spoken words can sometimes have different meanings by the way they sound. How do you sound? How do you write? Study yourself, learn how others perceive you and then make the necessary corrections.

When evaluating ourselves, we must take a look at what we believe, how we react in stressful situations, and especially how we are motivated or become excited and enthusiastic about doing a certain task. What is our confidence level? Are we easily distracted?

Again, there are many outlets to improving our mental abilities. There is counseling. Sometimes we need an objective third party to help us determine why we act or behave in a certain manner. They can help us explore ways to make the necessary changes we want to make. There are seminars, self-help and motivational books (like this one), audio and video tapes. Zig Ziglar, Dale Carnegie and Steven Covey and many other well-respected motivators have built an entire industry on the self-help phenomenon. The Bible and/or other religious books, based on whatever our religious or fundamental beliefs might be, can guide us through certain situations.

Again, the trick is to identify our mental strengths and weaknesses, determine which part of our mental make-up may be holding us back or impacting us negatively, and then find a way to change our behavior.

Mental is the playing field, and mental is the level at which we can and are willing to play. It is important to realize the best possible fit for our individual ambitions. It's okay, and even desirable, to set goals a little high, as long as we are realistic and know when to back off.

Improving our abilities is about being the best we can be. It's a never-ending process that lasts throughout our lives. Each victory and failure helps us in immeasurable ways. The important thing is to understand that life is all about learning and growing and moving forward with a positive mindset. As entrepreneur Kemmons Wilson says, "There are two ways to get to the top of an oak tree. One way is to sit on an acorn and wait for it to grow. The other way is to climb an oak tree that has already grown."

Think of improving your abilities as climbing an oak tree. Look back now and again to see how far you've come, but never take your eye off the top.

3
Make Your First Impression A Good One

I follow a few simple rules to help me try to make a good first impression. First, it's imperative that you conduct yourself in a manner that is friendly and pleasant. Be kind and greet everyone with a handshake and a smile. Look the person in the eye and repeat their name when it's given.

The courtesy of interaction with everyone with whom you have contact should never be less considerate or respectful, regardless of who they are, their stature, position or wealth. None of these should make one bit of difference. You never know when someone you think of as insignificant may turn out to be a person of power, wealth or position.

There is a story of the miner/rancher/land owner who appeared at the registration desk of the beautiful Antler's Hotel in Colorado Springs and asked for a room. He was dirty and unkempt in appearance and looked as though he had nothing. He was refused a room. This individual was very wealthy. He owned gold mines, cattle, land and had the ability and assets to build his own hotel.

Understandably irritated and angered, he went down the road and built the magnificent BROaDMOOR Hotel. This hotel has become the toughest competitor to the Antler's.

When designing the sign and choosing the peculiar spelling of the name Broadmoor he used all capital letters except for one. The "a" in Broadmoor is always a small "a" supposedly to show his resentment for his treatment at the Antler's.

What would have happened if he had been given a room at the Antler's? Maybe the BROaDMOOR wouldn't be there. So, it is better to treat people properly, especially if you are in business. Remember everyone is a potential customer or maybe a competitor.

Second, if you're going into an environment that requires a certain type of dress, you should adjust to that. Today's workplace is becoming more casual, but it is still important to dress appropriately. For example, a corporate atmosphere will most likely have persons dressed in business suits or business attire. Even if you are a contractor and work in jeans at all your job sites, it is important to put on a suit if you are going to visit a potential corporate client.

Have a positive physical appearance. Be well groomed. Pay attention to good hygiene. Make certain your hair is combed or styled, your hands and nails are clean and your breath smells good. We all have different looks and have different physical statures and weight. Some of us are skinny. Some aren't. Some of us have receding hairlines, some of us don't. However, anyone can have a positive physical appearance by practicing good hygiene, being well groomed and dressing appropriately.

Try not to have preconceived notions about the people you meet. One time I was at a public affair where there were many different people. I saw a group of folks who were standing next to some Harley Davidson motorcycles. They looked rough, tough and mean with scraggly beards and sleeveless shirts. My first impression was to stay away from them. However, I like motorcycles. I don't ride one on the highway or streets and never wanted my children to ride street bikes, but we rode dirt bikes. Motorcycles aren't necessarily dangerous, but they are hard to see by motorists and I feared my children might be hurt. I am also a firm believer in helmets. Anyway, I approached the motorcycle riders and struck up a conversation. They were some of the nicest people I have ever met. If I had responded only to my first impression, I wouldn't have had the opportunity to visit with them and I would have missed out on what I consider to be a positive experience.

Don't try to force your opinion on others. It is difficult to convince someone your opinion is better than theirs. If you have an open mind and listen to someone else's opinions, you might learn something and you might change your own mind. It is okay to hold different opinions than others, but have as much respect for their opinions as you would like them to have of yours.

Look in the mirror and say, "How would I react if someone approached me the same way I am approaching them?" Judge yourself honestly. Also, listen to constructive criticism from others.

Most important of all, be <u>sincere</u>. The impression you leave is not only conduct, behavior patterns and appearances, it is also sincerity. People can spot a phony a mile away. I have always had a good relationship with small children because they have great intuition. They know when someone is sincere and when someone is not. It is hard for an adult to fool a child. It seems to be an innate trait that kids really pick up on the kind of individual they're dealing with. Many times we adults lose that intuition because we are eager to look for either the best in a person or the worst. We have preconceived ideas.

If you're superficial or conducting yourself in a certain manner just to impress someone, it will show. We must continually monitor our personal skills. We need to develop behavior patterns that make good impressions.

Not Everyone Will Like You

You may find this hard to believe, but some people just are not going to like you! You may make a wonderful impression on 95% of the people with whom you deal. Still, there is going to be that 5% out there that won't like you no matter what you do.

One of the toughest things I had to learn in life was that everyone wasn't going to like me. I was devastated when I heard someone didn't like me, especially if I liked them and hadn't done anything to them. I once had a close friend whose brother intensely disliked me...and he'd never even met me! These brothers had a discussion about me and my friend told his brother, "Hey, you're mistaken, Gene's a good guy." This may have helped because when the brother and I finally got acquainted, we eventually became friends.

This brother had a preconceived notion about me before he even met me. That happens. Some people will have built-in resentment or conceptions about you. If you are successful, they may resent that. If you are handsome (I'm not), they may resent that. If you're an athlete, a professor, a newspaper editor or a lawyer, some people won't like you. Maybe you remind them of someone else they don't like and they base their dislike on that, judging you before they give themselves a chance to find out that you are nothing like the person they dislike.

These impressions can be overcome, if you conduct yourself in such a manner that these people can see you are sincere, honest and not egocentric.

We Are All Human. Sometimes, We Blow It!

It happens time and time again. A professional football coach lets loose at a referee with expletives, and it's picked up by a television camera. An evangelist succumbs to human weaknesses and is caught. A politician, under a lot of stress, makes a public relations gaffe and it's headlines all over the world.

It's hard to be perfect. In fact, it just can't be done. Many of the people I'm talking about make very good impressions most of the time. But, sometimes, they mess up. And, if you're in the limelight, your error seems particularly glaring. How many of us would like to be held up to the kind of scrutiny to which famous people are subjected? Could we measure up?

I believe there are peaks and valleys in how we feel and how we conduct ourselves on a daily basis. There are times you don't feel well or are irritable. For whatever reason, we blow it. When you do something you are not proud of, the best thing to do is to own up to the mistake. If you've insulted someone or hurt them, make contact and tell them you are sorry and that you made a mistake. Be truly apologetic. That is about all you can do. The person may or may not accept your apology. Most people will, if you are sincere.

There are variations of giving and forgiving. Some of us are more lenient and condoning than others. Relatives and close friends often become so angry with each other that the wound never heals and bonds are broken for long periods of time. We sometimes become remorseful and feel a need to overlook the past, forgive, or "make-up" without ever discussing the incident that caused the split. Some of us are more indulgent than others. Some of us are less sensitive and try to overlook statements or actions that others find offensive.

The best way to live your life is to try to understand that people say and do things that they don't mean. Their emotions and stress levels are high and they are not themselves when you see them or hear of their actions. Being tolerant will carry you a lot further than getting easily offended. Compassion and the understanding that sometimes, if we overlook things that offend us, we will avoid hard feelings and arguments or permanent damage to relationships that are important to us.

Now that I've said that, let me tell you that I realize *some things* are unforgivable. For example, I will never buy a Kansas City Star newspaper because of the innuendoes and half-truths that I feel are published in that paper. When I ran for Governor of Kansas, I was invited to meet with the editorial board. Only half of them bothered to show up, in "their" building. Most of them left in a few minutes. I don't think they heard a word I said. They had their minds made up with pre-conceived ideas and never bothered to learn about me or my ideas. I thought their articles were biased and slanted. I feel the same about the Rose's, who own the county newspaper there, as well. The Wichita Eagle was somewhat the same way but they improved with time. All the other newspapers in the state I felt were fair and followed the rules of good journalism.

On the other hand, I have had differences with friends and relatives and have "broken the ice" by my initiative because I want to be a forgiving person and I want to be forgiven. My friend, Dr. John K., once teed me off (my fault) and I got angry. He never did. He wouldn't be offended by me. Later, I told him I was wrong and thanked him for remaining my friend. I also told him he was a better and bigger man than I was for preserving our friendship. Dr. Glenn H. and I have remained friends through a rocky experience where resentment could have lasted a lifetime.

Friendships are valuable. Don't lose them over a misunderstanding. Walt Mc, Bill K, Howard W., Bill R. (deceased), Mickey C., Gene R., Ulie C., Jim K., Jean & Jim Mc, all classmates and many others from classes before and after me in Baxter Springs High School have kept in touch through the years. I marvel at the stability in all those classes. Long employment, stable family life, strong faith, and loving caring people. It's always a pleasure to see those individuals and renew old memories.

Whenever you think about ending a friendship or family relationship look deep in your heart and ask yourself if you really want to lose this person from your life. Wouldn't it be much more meaningful and rewarding to be forgiving?

It can be a frightening and humbling experience to have to apologize or own up to a blunder. You never know how people will react. It is a time when you are at your most vulnerable. I've had disagreements with friends. I've gone to them and said, "We've been friends too long to let one single incident come between us. I want to ask you to forgive me for anything I said that hurt you and I want you to know that I forgive you for what you said that hurt me. I'd like to salvage our relationship, and I promise to try not to offend you anymore."

It may take some time for the hurts to heal. But, the first and hardest step is to apologize. Some of the most difficult things to do are the things we feel better about when we've done them.

Interviewing Is An Art

The art of interviewing is the ability to make a positive impression by appearance, articulation and mannerisms at the start of the interview and to continue in an intellectual way through the end.

Many positions are lost by the very best and most capable candidates because they don't know how to interview. Be yourself. Being at ease and not trying to be someone or something you are not is the first step. Know your strengths and discuss them and your willingness to learn. Most of all, stress your desire to do a good job and be a positive part of the team.

First, appearance is important. Shoes, socks, neat and clean attire is a must. Hair should be neat and fingernails trimmed and properly presented.

Second, confidence and friendliness is important. Your voice should project an air of confidence. If you are unsure or un-knowledgable about something, say so, but express your desire to learn. Be a fast learner.

Third, be prepared with knowledge about the position for which you are being interviewed. Try to find out as much as possible about what's happened historically with the company. Talk to former employees or people currently working for the company. Try to know what they are looking for and what they expect. It's okay to ask these questions during the interview.

Fourth, look for problems you may encounter immediately if you take the job. Ask questions that are pertinent to that problem and have potential solutions in mind to solve them. Show an understanding and knowledge about why you are being interviewed. Make certain the interviewer knows you have a high level of interest. Listen carefully to what they say and try to get the interviewer to talk as much as possible, especially about the job.

Fifth, keep good eye contact and listen well. Be certain you have covered what the interviewer wants to cover. Ask the interviewer if you've answered the questions to his or her satisfaction. If you show high interest, it's easy to get information that may be valuable.

Sixth, sell yourself. Be sure they know your strengths and best qualities. Express how interested you are and that you'll do your best, work hard and give 110% if given the opportunity.

Seventh, be careful about bragging about your accomplishments. Characterize your accomplishments in terms that don't sound too egotistical. Let the interviewer know that you can handle responsibility. Express how challenge motivates you and how being a part of a successful team and company is your goal and aspiration. Explain your ability to get along with people and that handling stress and complex issues is part of your forte.

Physical characteristics do play a role in the interview process, but a proper presentation can gain and overcome any physical characteristics that don't present themselves well. Actions, knowledge and people skills are great assets in influencing people.

Some Behavior is Definitely Off-Limits

Down to earth people are pleasant to be around. They make you feel comfortable in their presence. They're not pretentious or cavalier. Somewhere between being common folk and assuming your prestige you have to maintain some sophistication level that avoids personal inferences and offhand remarks that imply something that might be taken personally.

It is definitely improper to comment on an associate's physical appearance or to flirt with them in a manner which could be interpreted to be sexual.

One of my associates, while we were at a dinner with clients, made a crude comment to a young man in our group. Luckily, his comment didn't offend anyone but it could have. People are more casual about joking and making off-color remarks these days. However, it is important to develop a level of sophistication to know when NOT to make such comments. It is always wise to refrain from such comments in a business setting, even if you're friendly and know your other associates well. It's just good sense to refrain from comments or jokes about race, politics or sex. In addition to offending someone, you may leave yourself open for a sexual harassment claim over something that you intended very innocently.

In today's working environment, the government has made it easy for EEOC claims to be made for discrimination, harassment and unfair practices. To be honest, some of these claims are fair and just. But, unfortunately, may of them are not. And, like it or not, in these situations you are assumed guilty until proven innocent and by then the damage to your reputation is already done. Any time this happens, it is counterproductive to the business because we lose employees' time to court hearings, have to pay attorneys' fees, expenses and costs for the charges. An employee can go to a government office, file a claim of discrimination or sexual harassment, sign a form and they (for no charge) will be provided legal counsel. Whether the claim is legitimate or not, the company has to hire their attorney, lose valuable and productive time from their supervisors and managers as they go to hearings and meetings to defend the claim. We may win almost all of the cases but we have still lost a great deal of money unfairly.

It is important for business people to develop a level of sophistication in the workplace so they use good judgment in dealing with employees. Sophistication doesn't mean being a stuffed shirt or going around with your nose in the air. It is just knowing when to avoid making wise remarks that can get you in trouble. If you say something that the person or persons feel they have to respond to or defend, then you've probably said the wrong thing.

Whether you are an employee or supervisor, it is important to know that any claim of sexual harassment either by you or against you hurts your business. I believe many sexual harassment situations can be handled without the courts and the legal process if common sense and reason are used. If a man or woman in the workplace is approached in a sexually suggestive manner, either directly or indirectly, there is an opportunity to face the situation with discretion and intelligence.

First, if you are in a position in which you feel offended or threatened by another employee or a supervisor, you should deal with the offender directly. You should state very matter-of-factly that this behavior is inappropriate and you will not tolerate it. You must be very clear on this point. Many times that's the end of the situation and business can go on as usual.

However, if the behavior continues to persist, then it is time to get a supervisor involved. If you're the supervisor they come to, you must be very sensitive to this situation. It's a good idea to have policies and procedures in place to deal specifically with this type of problem. In fact, in today's working environment, it is imperative, and that means in *writing* and in a *policy* manual.

Too many times, a crisis that develops or the negative rhetoric that unravels in this kind of situation should never get to that stage. If it does, then the company or business has failed in their personnel policies mission.

Remember, if you are in a position of authority over any other person, you are at risk of being accused of being unfair or discriminatory. So, presenting yourself as sophisticated and professional at all times is essential. Not only must you be above reproach, you must also give the appearance of being above reproach.

5
Inherent Versus Learned
How Do We Become What We Become?

Are people born with certain traits and characteristics that shape their whole life? Is our life pre-destined from birth and life's experiences merely an accoutrement to what we eventually become? Are some people born smart? Some born lazy? These are age-old questions. Philosophers, academicians and even physicians have spent years on this subject and still the evidence is inconclusive.

Some contend that a newborn comes in the world with a clean slate. Her experiences and her environment provide the writings to fill that slate. If this is true, then how do we explain a child who grows up in a poor family with uneducated or abusive parents going on to become the President of our country, or a famous personality, or a successful business person?

Common sense and logic lead me to believe that a person is shaped both by her inherent traits and by her life experiences. Unfortunately, too much of either can cancel the other out. For instance, if a child has an inherent trait of intelligence, but is born into an environment that never affords her the opportunity to grow intellectually, then she may never have a chance.

Inherent traits are an important part of one's personality. We develop certain traits as we go through life, and those traits become an integral part of us. However, we are also shaped by other influences in our lives.

When I think of inherent traits, I can't help but think about dogs. While it may be difficult to detect or pinpoint in a human being exactly what is an inherent trait and what is a learned trait, it is fairly easy to pinpoint inherent traits in dogs.

I've had several dogs in my lifetime and some of them have been really great dogs. I remember each of them for their different personalities and their temperaments. While it is true that dogs can learn, much of their makeup is due to heritage or bloodline and this leads me to believe that people have inherent traits in much the same way.

For instance, I remember Max, a German Shepherd we once had. Max was full grown and had apparently been through some obedience training. Somehow he got separated from his owner. He showed up at my brother's drive-in restaurant one day. Max would not let anyone there get close to him but he would take food the employees gave to him. My brother placed an ad in the local newspapers but to no avail. After a few days, when there had been no response, he called me. He knew I wanted a German Shepherd.

I drove the 30 miles to my brother's place to see this dog. Mysteriously, as soon as the dog and I saw each other, we bonded. On sight, we were together! I took him home and my wife and the kids accepted him immediately. Now, Maggie, our mixed breed, was a different story. She growled, challenged him and stood facing the dog food bag, guarding it with her life. When Maggie finally realized that Max was staying, she grudgingly accepted him.

Ironically, Max later saved Maggie's life. Even though neither of them had ever shown more than tolerance for each other, the incident proved there was some kind of tie.

It was a cold winter evening, after sunset, and the ground was frozen hard. The temperature hovered around the 3° mark. We lived in the country and had three barns, a chicken house (no chickens at the time) and a couple other outside buildings. The dogs were still outside.

Max began barking and carrying on in that nervous way dogs will when something isn't right. We went to the back door to see what the commotion was all about. Max started barking again and ran towards the outbuildings. We watched him for a few minutes, and when we didn't follow, he came back and barked rapidly again and started running off in the other direction once more. We realized he wanted us to follow him, so we did. He led us to the chicken house where he began trying to dig under the house. I noticed his paws were almost raw. I got down on my stomach and looked under the building. There was Maggie, wedged under the floor. She had apparently chased something under there and got stuck. She could barely make a sound by the time we found her. She would not have lived through the night if Max hadn't brought us to her. We jacked up the building and set her free. A hot meal and hero's accolades were in line for Max. Maggie settled for a warm place and the meal.

Max was later killed in an accident, but I remember him for his loyalty. I don't know why he took to me the way he did. I like to think something in his nature understood something in mine. Max had a loyal personality. I believe I have that kind of personality. I believe that somehow Max understood that his loyalty to me would be rewarded, and it was. The way Max sensed certain things was a phenomenon. We could communicate and he tried his best to please me. We were inseparable. When I was away on business he got to stay in the house with Marie and the kids. Somehow when I was coming home after being gone overnight or on a trip that lasted several days he seemed to sense my arrival. It wasn't as if I arrived at a scheduled or even predictable time each evening. Sometimes I had driven hundreds of miles, but he would begin pacing in front of the door about 30 minutes or so before I got home. He seemed to know I was coming.

King, an English Setter, was another one of the outstanding dogs by which I've had the pleasure of being owned. King was four years old when I got him and had been trained by his previous owner. He was a hunting dog. As a hunting dog, he had the required trait of obedience. We enjoyed many hunts together.

Bird dogs are usually kept in pens and not allowed to run free. The reason for this is that if they wander off hunting and go on point, they could remain there as long as their prey remains. They can also cover large areas and could easily become lost. So, the trait of obedience in a hunting dog is essential. In this manner they can be controlled and not lose their discipline.

King was different. In his later years, I could let him run free, but he never lost his discipline on a hunt. He was also different than most bird dogs in that he was housebroken. I would bring him inside with me, and he would sleep all night next to my bed and never mess in the house. He was a great companion and friend. Because bird dogs are kept in pens, they have to learn to go to the "bathroom" where they live. That's the reason it's so unusual for them to know they can't go in the house.

One day J.B., Terry (father and son, and friends of mine) and I were going quail hunting. Delores, Jay's wife, packed us a lunch. She made six sandwiches with all the trimmings and dessert. I didn't pay much attention and we somehow put the lunch in the back of the camper with King. He ate all the lunch, including the dessert, with the exception of one peanut butter and jelly sandwich Dory had filled in with, the other five sandwiches were ham and cheese. The hunters were good sports about it, but we reminded Dory the next time that she shouldn't make any peanut butter and jelly sand-wiches because King didn't like them.

We all hunted many times after that and King made it up to them by being a good bird dog. Some people are like that too. They goof sometimes, but they find a way to make up for their mistakes.

Max II was a Doberman Pincher. He was given to me as a pup by Doyle and Velma, friends who live in Chicago. He was a red Doberman, with a gentle nature, something which people don't necessarily equate with a Doberman. In fact, the night watchman's pit bull used to rough Max II up a bit while he was growing up.

He was one of the few dogs I actually raised from a pup. The second day I got him home, he fell in the swimming pool and I had to rescue him. He was completely under the water.

His eyes were big as dollars when he looked up at me. He was paddling like mad when I lifted him out, and he never left my side the rest of the day.

Max II disappeared after he had been with us about eighteen months. I have often wondered if his gentle nature contributed to his disappearance. After all, most people are cautious around Dobermans, but Max II was so gentle. He would go off with anyone. There was a pack of wild dogs where we lived and they may have killed him. Or, he may have been run over by our helper and we weren't told. At any rate, we were sad that we missed the full potential of Max II.

My fourth favorite and current dog is Shadow, a Golden Retriever. She was originally named McKenzie by our grandchildren, but we changed her name to Shadow after seeing the movie "Homeward Bound." Shadow is an ornery lady. We got her for our grandkids as a Christmas gift. They had her for a year, through those difficult puppy stages. Obedience training and house destruction were out of the way when we were given the dog. Shadow was and still is sometimes hyperactive. She wasn't getting enough individual attention with the kids in school and sports. When anyone would show her any interest, she'd go wild.

With Rita away during the week, Shadow and I had a lot of time together in the evenings. She now minds pretty well, but still likes to play. She has become an integral part of our family and a positive influence in our lives. She loves attention and responds to it with love and devotion. What more could you ask of a dog? She likes to play rough and chew on me but she never chews on Rita. She knows what's acceptable and what's not. She still goes wild when the kids show up and she wants to be a part of any company we have. She is so social that she will go from one visitor to another, if more than one, giving equal attention to each person. She can communicate well with us and lets us know if she has a crisis or is someone is around or she wants something.

It is interesting to me, as I think about these dogs, how their nature or their inherent traits are similar to traits in people. Dogs are like friends and employees. We have a few outstanding ones, a few better-than-average ones and a few mediocre ones. They possess certain traits and talents which must be developed and nurtured. Part of that nurturing can take place by interaction with people around them. Those who care for and train dogs help them hone and improve their personalities and traits.

All people have a nature, a temperament or personality of some kind. But, we are social creatures, and we need the interaction with others to hone and improve our own talents and skills. Artists can learn from studying other artists. Writers and poets read the works of other writers and poets. Dancers study under other dancers. And, successful people like to be around and study other successful people.

When you encounter an example of success that you have to compete with, you are forced to compare yourself to others. It is not hypothetical any more. You are in the presence of something done well and now you have to compare. Attitude takes over and you keep practicing or studying until you get better and better.

I was a journeyman meat cutter at the age of 18. This was back in the days when customers picked their meat out of the display case and their selection was wrapped and tied with string or tape. I was pretty impressed with my skill at wrapping meats and filling customer orders. My older brother hired me to work in his shop on Saturdays. Much to my surprise, he was twice as fast as I was. I was truly astonished that I was not as good as he was. I was determined to get better and I did, but our time of working together wasn't long enough for me to master the skills to his level. I became better because of him. The better the people around us, the more challenged we are to improve.

While in the Army at Fort Leonard Wood, I boxed and played football. Everyone was drafted in those days; this included highly-skilled athletes. There were many great athletes in our unit. Surrounded by them, my athletic skills looked even better. You always look better than you are when you are surrounded by great players.

One of the great experiences Rita and I have enjoyed is to watch and be a part of the great sea turtles coming back to the beach they were born on and laying their eggs. We have gone out during the night and watched them come onto the beach. If they are disturbed they will return to the ocean and wait for another night. When they come in to the beach they go to a high spot in the sand and build their nest and then camouflage it to protect against predators. We watched patiently and when all is just right the turtle goes into a trance and lays her eggs. They have tears running down their face. As any birth, it is strenuous and very tiring on the mother. Once the eggs have been deposited there is the laborious task of returning to the sea.

The amazing thing about this process is that they never forget where they came from or who they are. They travel thousands of miles to return to their roots. All we humans have to do is <u>remember</u> and <u>be humble</u>. The bigger our head gets, the easier it is to fill our shoes.

Those who are successful in their careers know their strengths and weaknesses. They surround themselves with team members, employers and employees who enhance their strengths. Sometimes it's a long struggle to get to the point where we are secure in our strengths and able to deal with our weaknesses. Sometimes you even get knocked down and have to get up and start over.

That's when your inherent traits, whatever they are, play a major role in determining your future. You have to have some kind of desire or flame within to keep you moving on track and ahead.

If you believe that successful people haven't had their trials and tribulations, you're wrong. No one gets through this life unscathed. We all have correction opportunities. Setbacks, fears, stress, anxieties, and tough times come to rich and poor alike. Arguments, conflicts, confrontations, disagreements, pressures from family, finances and lawsuits are a part of everyone's experience. It's how we learn to deal with the negative. We must improve our ability and desire to learn how, in what way, and where to deal with these negatives.

6
Have a Little Compassion

From the time I was twelve years old until I was in my mid-30's, I never cried. I was taught that you had to be tough. You could beat me, but I wouldn't shed a tear, at least when someone was watching. That was how I was raised. Men didn't cry. It was rough and tumble times.

I was raised in a mining community where men labored hard in the mines and women labored hard at home. We washed clothes by hand with a washboard and a big tub. We cleaned linoleum or wood floors by hand. Family clothing was sewn from whatever cloth you could get, usually flour sacks that had been bleached and dried. Life was hard but simple. There was no television and few radios, so entertainment consisted of social gatherings with friends and family. Visiting, playing cards or picnicking was the usual Sunday schedule since everyone worked a six-day week. Family gatherings were frequent and visiting was the entertainment.

On Saturday, after everyone was paid, people would gather downtown to walk the streets, see friends and talk. In Picher, Oklahoma, it was not uncommon for some of these talks to become forceful. It was also not uncommon to see two grown men, with different points of view, get into a fist fight on the street . People would form a circle around them and cheer on their favorite as the two slugged it out. Fighting with your fists was the way to settle disputes and disagreements. Lawsuits and lawyers were not prevalent, actually they were non-existent. No law enforcement was available in most cases. Town constables and justices of the peace were about all there was with which to contend. It was the survival of the fittest.

In those days, the miners had big families. After all, they would go to bed at dark and wake up at daylight with nothing else to do for the couple of hours before they had to go to work. My dad always told me I would have been a lot older if he hadn't been so bashful.

Hard work and honesty ruled the day. Kids fought for dominance, much like animals do, to establish who was toughest. That really wasn't that long ago. Look how much things have changed. A fist fight on the street today would bring at least six policeman and automatic assault charges and court cases, if not time in jail.

I lived in that "rough and tough" cycle for quite some time. It wasn't until I had my own family and began building a business that I learned that slugging it out isn't the best way to solve a problem. I also learned that other people have feelings, desires and dreams just like I do. And, they want them respected.

Showing your compassion isn't a sign of weakness. In my mind, it is actually a sign of strength. Somewhere in my mid-30's, I learned to cry again. I can't recall the exact incident but I'm not embarrassed by it. I make no excuses for my tears. Actually, I am proud of the fact that I have emotions and can show them. If I am reading the newspaper, or hear about a heinous crime, particularly if it involves children, I tend to cry. Also, if I hear a heart-warming story, or watch a sad or happy movie I might cry.

A friend of mine recently called to tell me about her son and daughter-in-law who had finally been able to adopt a child. During this process, I had been involved in trying to help them find a child and knew how much they wanted one. The tears were slushing down my face pretty freely when my wife walked in the room and became alarmed.

"What's wrong?", she asked.

"Nothing. I'm just happy!", I replied.

When I think about it, the rough times early in this century can't compare to the rough times we have today. Although toughness ruled the day, meanness and evil weren't as apparent as they are now. When I look at the news and see our country being victimized by terrorists, some of whom are our own Americans, I can't help but think our country is losing its conscience, its compassion and its moral compass. History has shown us other countries where leaders rule through cruelty and fear. But here in the United States we have always put ourselves above that mentality.

For the longest time, I believed we held the moral high ground. Not anymore. How have we come to the place where we have so little value for human life? Our children are starting to kill each other. When a six-year-old beats a month-old baby to death, you know that child just doesn't understand the value of human life. I can't help but wonder who failed to teach this child compassion.

Don't ever lose compassion. Don't think of compassion or emotion as a sign of weakness. Don't make apologies and don't have regrets for feeling compassion toward your fellow human beings. After all, as thinking, feeling human beings, it's nearly impossible to throw compassion completely out the window. It's a vital ingredient in our moral make-up. The opposite of compassion is apathy. If we begin to let indifference be a part of our moral make-up, chaos will certainly rule the day.

154

PART IV

LEADERSHIP CREATES SUCCESS

1
Motivating Our People To Want To Succeed

It takes vision, leadership and courage to make a business succeed. Leadership is the prime difference between success and failure. Leaders think long term and grasp the big picture. They arm themselves with strong values and discipline while being courageous and commanding respect and commitment. A leader must be able to focus on the important, not the unimportant, to find simple answers to complex questions.

A leader also has to have a team to lead. A leader knows she can't do the job alone. She has to have good people working with her (note that I didn't say "for" her) to accomplish the goals of the team. While the leader can look ahead to potential opportunities and challenges, she has to know her team is taking care of the details and the tasks at hand.

Representative Behavior

The skills we learn out of necessity become deeply ingrained in our psyche. If we have to get along with someone because our future or livelihood depends on it, we will usually force ourselves to find a way to live harmoniously with that person or persons.

The sooner in life we discover that some people affect our lives and success, the sooner we start developing behavior and habits that are acceptable to those with whom we must interact. Learning to adjust to others' expectations is usually controlled by our career or job position. We learn how the boss wants the job done, and we do it the way the boss wants it done!

However, if you are the boss, you have to develop the kinds of skills that encourage people to follow your lead and do the job the way you want it done. Just having the position of boss isn't enough to command respect among workers anymore. It is important to be as agreeable and flexible as you can without compromising the job or the company.

People learn by representative behavior. They learn through both positive and negative influences. Remember Pavlov's dogs? They learned through negative reinforcement. I was several years old before I found out my name wasn't "Damnit Gene."

"Damnit Gene, why did you start that fire?"

"Damnit Gene, where have you been?"

"Damnit Gene, I told you not to do that!"

When people called me just "Gene" they thought I was ignorant for not responding.

Leaders gain more ground by using positive influences to elicit certain behavior than they do by using negative influences. Negative influences (punishment or reprimand) are sometimes necessary, but they should be used as a last resort.

Some Leaders are Born. Some are Made

How you present yourself is vital to improving your career. People who are promoted are generally self-assured, confident, have a good track record of success, can demonstrate the ability to work well with other people and have a focus or goal.

Some people seem to be born with leadership capabilities. They have strong personalities, commanding voices, or a natural academic or athletic ability. These people automatically attract attention. Sometimes they don't have the most talent, but there's a certain charisma about them that inspires others to follow. These people have a head start.

Then, there are other people who have a lot of talent, education and thinking skills but they don't *automatically* command attention. This kind of leader has to work very hard on his personality and his ability to command attention.

I said some leaders are born. But I do know that leaders can be made because I'm that kind of leader. I don't think I gather a lot of attention in an initial encounter, so I have to work harder at presenting myself. In my case, I have to lead by example. I try to lead by being a hard worker, a caring listener and a sincere person. Establishing a track record of success sets a good example, which in turn attracts attention.

Lighting the Fire

Leaders have to understand the many techniques of motivation. Most people are motivated by one or all of the following: Money, Recognition, Personal Satisfaction or Power.

The challenge of leadership is learning what makes people react as they do. Each person has motivational forces. People also have a way of disguising their true personalities. Therefore, it becomes a challenge to find the spark in people that will ignite their desire to work hard and achieve their ambitions.

Finding the right niche for each person requires careful thought and study. We have to observe employees and be in tune with their lives. Too many managers live in glass houses and only see the world from their own viewpoint. A leader has the capability of seeing much further. It requires a nurturing and sincere personality.

Money, Money, Money

Many times managers automatically assume that money is the only motivational force behind an employee's ambitions. Of course, most employees expect to be paid a fair and competitive wage. But several studies have shown that money in itself is seldom a motivating factor in an employee's job satisfaction. However, it is important to pay employees a competitive wage based on the job description, the industry standard and the area in which you're doing business.

Wage studies and comparisons need to be examined and constantly updated. As businesses and industries try to operate more efficiently, it becomes imperative they have a good understanding of just how much their personnel expenses are and what the long-range personnel expense expectations are.

For example, wages in larger cities differ greatly from rural areas. Normally, the cost-of-living in rural areas is much lower than in metropolitan areas. If you are doing business in a resort or tourist area, cost-of-living expenses are going to be even higher. Businesses need to take the time to do wage comparisons within a 100-mile radius of where they are doing business. They must also examine the wages in competitors' businesses in their local area.

In order to offer a competitive wage, a good rule-of-thumb is to try to pay employees a wage that is somewhere between the highest wage paid in general and the lowest wage paid in your own community. For example, if your competitor locally is paying a data entry person $6.50 per hour starting wage, and the highest wage paid for that job within your 100-mile radius is $12.50 per hour, you can probably be competitive by starting a data entry person at $7 per hour. Then you need to take it a step further and plan on topping that employee's wage at $12.50 per hour.

You should explain to the potential data entry employee that you will begin her salary at $7 per hour. As of the date of employment, she can expect her top wage to be $12.50. Now we know that cost-of-living expenses will most likely rise before that employee reaches the $12.50 mark. This is why wage studies and comparisons need to be constantly evaluated, probably at least every two years. That follow-up evaluation might show that two years after her employment, she could expect her top wage to be $13.50. It is very important that the employee understand these numbers are not promises, only a guideline to let them know where they stand in their wage expectations.

Providing employees this information helps give them an understanding of how your business is competing for good employees. If your business shows an honest effort to stay competitive, then that gives employees a sense of satisfaction in regard to their wages. They know they can probably make more money by moving to another location, but if they feel they are being compensated fairly in the business they work for, in the town where they live, they are more likely to stay long-term employees.

Employees also need to know that your cost of employing them is far more than what they actually see in wages. They need to understand just how much their benefits are worth and how much those benefits cost. These benefits might be a company car or car allowance, insurance benefits, or a retirement plan, social security, workers compensation, etc. An employee says, "Yes, I want those benefits. They are important to me," but they don't consider them to be a part of their pay. Employees see these as intangible and that has to change. Giving them this information provides employees a better understanding of how the business is working to keep them employed and why profit is so important to them keeping their jobs.

If an employee reaches his top-wage status, then he or the employer has to make a choice. That employee can work toward being promoted to a higher-paying position or seek a job with another company if monetary rewards are his only goal.

Recognition and Self-Satisfaction

Employees do a good or outstanding job every day. Employees go beyond the call of duty. Employees make the business a success.

Good leaders want to provide these types of employees with some kind of reward for their extra effort. It may not always be possible to reward an employee monetarily, other than overtime wages, for going that extra mile or for a consistently outstanding performance.

It's important to make employees feel special and appreciated for the work they do. Many times, a simple thank you from the boss will go a long way toward employee morale. Employees get a lot of personal satisfaction by feeling they've made a difference in the organization. Again, sincerity is important when thanking employees for doing a good job. You have to mean it. If you don't, your thanks will come off sounding hollow, and it will do little good toward motivating your workers.

Some businesses provide special monthly or quarterly recognition of employees. A picture and name on a plaque, prominently displayed in the office, lets others know that someone outstanding works for your organization.

Another way to thank employees and recognize them for their hard work is hosting a special lunch. You could order a pizza from Pizza Hut, or encourage employees to bring a pot luck meal. After the meal, take time to recognize the employees and say thank you.

A good leader must give credit where credit is due. If an employee you are supervising comes up with a good solution for a particular problem, make sure the other employees and senior level managers know of his contribution. As a leader, you must be confident enough not to be threatened by another's contribution. Remember, a leader is not judged solely on how well he does his job, but how well the entire team does their job.

I think back to my days as a supervisor at the tire manufacturing company. I asked my employees to help me learn and they responded. Our crew became known for our production levels. We got all the test runs because we were efficient. I asked for their help because they were good, and they knew it. You can encourage people to do their best if you are successful in stressing one basic point; if the company doesn't make a profit, then you aren't going to get a raise or more fringe benefits, because there won't be any money to provide those things.

The Power of Knowledge

Power can be a very useful tool placed in the proper hands. Power is an endowment of certain authority to an individual. Power can be easily abused, so you must be careful about who gets power in your organization.

Power, however, is a very motivating force for some people. When an employee is promoted to a supervisory position, that brings automatic power and responsibility. It gives an employee an opportunity to take more control over a situation than he or she perhaps had in the past.

Power doesn't only have to belong to the managers. Employees themselves can be empowered through good leadership. When an employee genuinely feels that he or she has some kind of control over the profitability of the company, that is a motivating factor.

Quality control or total quality management is a watchword of this generation. Total Quality Management (TQM) encompasses the belief that constant quality control throughout every aspect of the business will increase the profitability of that business. TQM is about empowering employees to guide and direct the profitability of the company.

In order to do this, leaders have to share knowledge with their employees. They have to train and retrain them at every opportunity. Leaders have to be vigilant in making certain their employees are watching the quality of their product or service right on down the line. Team management, team problem solving, involving the employees in planning projects and profit sharing programs help employees feel they are a very special force in the business. When workers know they are turning out a quality product, they can have pride in that product, and they know the profitability of the business and their personal profitability depends on them.

Employees who are empowered know their earning potential isn't determined subjectively by some unknown force sitting in an ivory tower somewhere at corporate headquarters. These employees have a good understanding of profit and loss margins and how they fit into the picture.

I have been amazed at the number of MBA students who didn't know the difference between Net Profit and Cash Flow. If our academic world doesn't cover the aspects of operational data, think how little we are informing our entire work force of the numbers necessary to go forward and at what pace.

2
Characteristics of Leadership

I've known many successful people in my lifetime, and I have identified a number of leadership characteristics that these people share. Many of these leaders have some or all of the characteristics. Of course, the more of these characteristics they possess, the better leaders they are.

A good leader is respected. Notice I didn't say liked. It's okay to be liked as a leader, but the most important things is to be respected. When I was in the military, a soldier under my supervision didn't show up on time, and I had to reprimand him. I took him aside and spoke to him about it. I heard later that he told others I had really chewed him out. Whey they asked him what I had said, he replied, "Well, he really didn't say very much, but he meant every word of it!" You don't want to leave negative feelings because people will resent you. The key is to get your point across in a way that others can understand and respect.

A good leader can remain calm. It's important to keep emotions out of any business situation, and it's also a hard thing to do. You must remain calm in an adverse situation. Others around you will be anxious, and a calm, composed leader can help put an adverse situation into perspective and keep the team on track.

A good leader has a sense of purpose. The challenge of a sense of purpose is to get all your employees focused on that purpose. That means you have to have a precise goal and a well-defined means of obtaining that goal. So, leadership doesn't always come in totality. It can come from a majority.

A good leader is persistent. You can't lose sight. You can't give up. And you can't give in. That's the difference between a leader and a dreamer. The leader will keep at it, keep at, keep at it. It takes patience, faith in yourself and hard work.

A good leader will sacrifice. Whining and complaining are out. Sometimes you'll have to give up your free time and miss social occasions to keep your business running smoothly. You can't brag when things are going well, either. A good leader doesn't go around always blowing his own horn. As we've said before, if you deserve credit, someone else will give it to you.

A good leader is a constant learner. Gaining knowledge will gain you position. The day you quit learning is the day you start slipping backwards. You must know your own strengths and weaknesses. You know what you do well, so concentrate on your strengths and try to improve your weaknesses.

A good leader is a good listener. You can't hear a thing over the sound of your own voice. A good leader knows the importance of observing and listening to others around him. A good leader is keen to the perceptions of her colleagues and employees. She is willing to be quiet and just take the time to listen to what others are saying.

A good leader garners confidence. People know this person can get the job done. When I was in Malaysia making a movie, I met a man who was believed to have special powers.

He was said to be able to predict the future. I came to know him well.

One time as I spoke to him, I noticed a lizard crawling on the ceiling. He said, "I will make that lizard fall." He seemed to make the lizard dizzy through his thought process and concentration. The lizard started running around in circles; his head dropped back, and I thought sure the lizard was about to fall. Instead, it excreted on the table below.

The man took his eyes away from the lizard and said, "The lizard hasn't done anything to me, so I will not hurt it."

I was telling this story to a large audience one time, and I held my hand out steadily to emphasize the power of listening. In the background, behind the stage, we could hear the sound of a motor running. I held my hand out for five or six seconds to a silent audience, and the motor suddenly quit running. I didn't have anything to do with it, but they might have believed I did if they had confidence in me.

A good leader knows the truth about her subordinates. The truth is, most subordinates resent their bosses or superiors. No matter how generous, forgiving, flexible, or lenient you are, many subordinates will harbor a resentment toward you. They may, however, never show it.

I have known a man for many years who always resented being second in command, but he couldn't take constructive criticism or suggestions very well. After he retired and felt safe, he took the opportunity to tell all his criticisms of what he perceived to be others' weaknesses. He cleared his harbored resentments and frustrations.

I didn't bother to respond or tell him I could match him point for point. Nor did I repeat other's negative opinions of him. That would have accomplished nothing and caused a greater difference. I simply said I heard his comments and registered them. I thanked him for expressing himself. <u>The mirror often registers a different reflection than what we're willing to accept.</u>

<u>A good leader takes charge of personal growth</u>. They have a solid understanding of their environment, their basic skills and knowledge of their profession. They're well informed and usually they are the best at what they do. They love their work and sincerely care about it. Their challenge is to be the best they can be-the best parent, the best professional person, the best human being.

<u>A good leader finds opportunity in adversity</u>. We all think we know ourselves, but we don't. You don't know how good you are, and you won't, until you put yourself to the test. Most people don't care how good they are because they have other things on their mind.

I think about Magic Johnson. When a recruiter was trying to get Magic to attend his university, he thought 7:00 AM would be a good time to catch him at home. He rang the bell and Magic's mother answered. "No, he's not here, he's on the court, shooting baskets and practicing," was her reply. Leading by hard work and example. He is one of our nation's best leaders. He sets an example by his presence. He's always smiling, friendly and he's good at what he does-playing basketball. But an outside influence, unrelated to his spectacular skills on the basketball court, caused Magic Johnson to look deep within himself and find some way to cope with being HIV positive and try to prevent others from becoming HIV.

Magic Johnson is still a leader, but now it is in the fight

against AIDS and the education of our young people to the dangers of unprotected sex. While he has definitely paid a high price for this role, it's a real break for our young people to have a national leader of Magic Johnson's caliber to help this cause.

A good leader possesses integrity and honor. Many people go through life getting their way and increasing their fortunes by deceiving people. They can be very good at it and get away with it for a long time. However, liars often have a hard time keeping up with all their lies, and sooner or later, they undo themselves. Look at Michael Milliken and other junk bond dealers. Where are they today?

Integrity is also important in business. Leaders must not only possess integrity, they must constantly give the appearance of possessing integrity. It is an ever-vigilant battle. Once a leader's integrity has been compromised, either by his own actions or actions of his subordinates, it is a difficult climb back up.

I learned my lesson about honesty and integrity the hard way. I had a neighbor who moved to Las Vegas and got a job as a guard in a casino. He was home for a visit one time and came to see me. He showed me a beautiful watch and said, "I'll sell it to you for a hundred dollars." I turned him down.

The next time he came to see me, he had a briefcase, a Polaroid camera and the watch. He needed money to get back to Vegas and he offered all of them to me for a hundred dollars. I said, "Okay, I'll buy them." I didn't have a nice watch. My partner Elmer and I split the cost of the merchandise. I got the watch.

Boy, was I proud of that watch. I was convinced I had gotten such a good deal. It had a gold band that was molded on to the face. One day, it stopped running, and I thought it probably just needed to be cleaned. I gave it to the jeweler, and he said, "Do you want me to clean this watch?"

"Yes, and if there's anything else it needs, go ahead and fix it."

"You want me to fix this watch?", he asked, as if he couldn't believe what I was asking him.

"Why? Shouldn't I?", I asked, now getting concerned.

"How much did you pay for it?"

"About $50. What's it worth?"

He smiled and said, "Oh they sell these by the dozen...for about $10 each."

I learned a valuable lesson about quality, honesty and integrity. Even though I got ripped off on the watch, the $50 I paid for it was worth the education.

We all have these kinds of experiences. Successful people are vulnerable to being overcharged regularly and frequently. I know many examples where I've been overcharged because "he can afford it." The price of service or merchandise can often be varied by what the market will bear. This will not change and if you get good service you probably won't say anything about it.

Everything in life is not fair. Bad health, bad luck, bad breaks, bad decisions or bad personalities can happen to anyone, anytime. (We may not be dealt good cards, but we have to play the hand dealt to us and do the best we can.)

3
There Is No "I" in the Word "Team"

"I built this company."

"I made this company what it is today."

"I AM the company."

"I brought this department up to its best production level in years."

How many times have you heard these kinds of statements from successful business people? They don't mean to be arrogant. And, they may not sound arrogant when they say it. An entrepreneur should be proud of his or her company and the company's accomplishments.

However, it usually takes more than one person to make a company or an organization successful. It takes teamwork. It takes a manager or an owner putting together a team of individuals who can build on progress and growth.

The most important asset for any business is the people...the people on the line working for their paychecks. Yet, the word "people" rarely shows up on a balance sheet or is figured into the company's worth. The most important asset we have and it's not on the financial statements, Profit and Loss, Balance Sheet, Cash Flow Statements or anywhere. Without the good people your company is questionable.

The best managers in business are those who can respect those people and inspire them to do their best. Everyone wants to be respected and to feel pride in themselves and their work, so the best managers are those who work like coaches, rather than dictators.

By now you have probably realized I use the "coach" analogy frequently. I think it is a good, healthy leadership role to play. Playing coach emphasizes the teamwork needed to achieve, respects the integrity of the individual and provides a motivating force for success.

Player Positions and Game Plans

There are two ways to build a team, you can fit the players to the game plan, or fit the game plan to the players. If you already have the game plan, a specific goal and a method for achieving it, then you want to fit the players to the game plan.

Analyze the people in your organization, find their strengths and weaknesses and determine which positions they should play. If you were coaching track, and you had a runner who couldn't do the 100 meters, but had a lot of stamina then you'd make him a distance runner. If you were a football coach and had a player with blazing speed, you wouldn't have him at the tackle position. Place your employees in the same way by thinking like a coach.

The same principles apply when hiring new employees or developing a new team. You need to know how you want your organization to look (your game plan), then you have to draft the players to fit into the organization. As in coaching, you need to look for depth in all your positions.

Since good employees are our most valuable assets, it is very competitive out there to find the right people. Good people command and demand the high salaries and top benefits because they are good. If they are good for one company, then another company will want them because it is so hard to find good people. Demand is high for good employees in service and trade industries.

Good people can come to you through the job opening and interview process, but I've found the best managers and senior-level people in my organization by looking at people doing similar jobs in other organizations.

Let me say right now that I have a prejudice. I never use "head hunters." We have never hired anyone through an employment service that is still with our company. Plus, it is very expensive. Potential employees who use "head hunters" are looking for a job for a reason. Those people who are doing a job well are usually paid well to do it. Those people doing a job well are usually so busy they don't have time to look for another job. The people who are doing a job well are occupied and happy enough with what they do on a daily basis that their thoughts aren't on moving on.

That does not mean that I don't hire someone who already works for another company but seeks employment with one of our organizations. It's just a factor that I keep in mind. I prefer to find these senior-level mangers through other opportunities.

You, as an employer might have something better to offer good people who are already doing excellent jobs for someone else. So, instead of looking at potential employees who are on the hunt for a new job, I go on the offense and hunt for employees who are already doing a good job.

Potential employees should have a good track record at their current jobs. They should have some kind of record of longevity. In today's employment environment, longevity can be subjective. Look at the resume. If a potential employee has held previous positions two to five years, that's a good track record. If their resume shows a continual advancement in responsibility from position to position, that's a positive indicator.

Observe the kinds of responsibility the potential employee has had in previous positions. Does this employee appear to be promotable? Remember, to build a successful team, you need depth in all positions. It's best to hire people you believe can move up in your organization over a period of time. Keep in mind that if you are able to lure an employee away from another company, that employee could be tempted to be lured away from YOUR company.

Do Some Research on Who You are Hiring

In today's litigious environment, it's becoming more difficult to get information on potential employees. You can't ask a potential employee anything about their personal life. You can't ask about their marital status or their personal habits. However, there are some tools at your disposal.

You can require blood tests. This has become a common practice because of the proliferation of drug use in our society and in the workplace. It is important that employees understand the reason behind doing blood or urine testing.

You can do a certain amount of background checking through public record sources. You can check police reports and you can run a credit check on a potential employee. You can also talk to his former employers.

Getting references from former employees isn't as easy as it used to be. Again, our litigious society prevents employers from giving negative statements about former employees. Some companies have instituted wholesale policies that they will not give references, good or bad.

However, it is still possible to get some reference information from most employers. Generally speaking, people don't want to hurt anyone else, and they will be hesitant if they cannot give a good recommendation. It is as important to listen to what you don't hear as it is to what you do hear.

How do you listen to what you don't hear? Make note of the things the potential employee or former employer doesn't talk about. One good question to ask a former employer is if they had the opportunity, would they hire their former employee again? Listen carefully to how they answer. If they give a resounding "yes" you can infer that the relationship was very positive. If they say, "Yes, but in some different category or assignment," that gives you information too. If they say "no" or, "I would rather not comment," you can infer that the relationship wasn't a positive one.

If possible, I also try to hire people with good morals and reputable character. Since I can't come out and ask a person about their personal lives, this is a difficult process. However, you can get some idea about a person's character through the legal means I mentioned earlier. You can find out if they have money problems. You can find out, many times from their resume, what civic activities they are involved in.

There is no sure-fire way to make certain you are getting the right employee when you go outside the company to find these people. As I've said before, your best people are probably already working in your company. If there is a way to promote from within, that is the best thing to do.

The following characteristics are what I look for in hiring employees;

- Visionary thinkers who aren't blinded by tunnel-vision and can plan their time well.
- Productive people capable of accomplishing and completing a goal.
- Ambitious people who are willing to earn their reward instead of just expecting it.
- Communicators who respect others' opinions and can take constructive criticism. People who will change their view point when presented a better suggestion.
- People who recognize the accomplishments of others and give credit where credit is due.
- People who understand that failure is a part of the learning process, and who grow professionally from past defeats.
- Individuals who calculate their productivity through real ity and utilize their time in an efficient manner.
- <u>Human beings who are not afraid to be accountable</u>.

Listening Helps Build the Team

If you call on others to help you, for instance in a decision-making process, record on paper all comments that are made so you don't forget. Even more importantly, this lets those speakers know they are being taken seriously. In such a situation, no one should dominate the conversation. Input should come from everybody, and once it's put together, you'll have a multitude of ideas to work with. Plus, employees who believe they make a difference in your company have a sense of worth and self-respect that is vital to your organization.

Remember, you hire employees to do a job. It is best to let them do their job without too much interference from you. That doesn't mean you don't provide guidance. It simply means you respect your employees' expertise.

"<u>Yes People</u>" Don't Help the Team Effort

We don't want people on our team who are going to agree with everything the coach says. We need a little disagreement now and then as a kind of check and balance. Some of the greatest ideas your organization will get may come from dissenters-people who don't agree with the accepted way of doing things.

If someone on your team disagrees with you, keep the lines of communication open. Discuss the disagreement; hammer it out until you come to a conclusion. There won't be any animosity if you keep the discussion related to the business situation at hand. People who disagree with you now and then are doing your team a service.

There is no such thing as smooth sailing all the time. If *two* people *always agree about everything, one of them is unnecessary.* You have to encounter a little rough water now and then. The long-term vision is to keep the ship on course through all kinds of waters. That's how we improve and grow.

Encourage Pride

For anyone to perform well in their job, they must have a sense of pride. As a coach, you must encourage pride in your team.

As a youngster working in the grocery store, I leaned how my own pride could make me work harder and better. One day, as I was stocking shelves, with my mind probably on other things, and perhaps not working as hard as I could, the manager, who was making up the weekly newspaper ad, called to me:

"Hey Gene, how should I fill up the last space in this ad?" I walked up and down the aisle, seriously considering each item. I picked one and said, "How about putting this in there?"

"Great idea!" he said, and added it to the ad. It didn't make that much difference to him what went in the ad, but it sure made a big difference to me. Boy, I felt proud, and the rest of the day, I worked twice as hard, with thoughts of some day being a manager of my own store.

Why not try to make people feel worthwhile? It's not only a good thing to do for personnel reasons, but it makes good business sense. Proud, happy people do better work. What does it cost to give a compliment?

I used to tell my children that their challenge was to be kind and friendly to everyone they encounter. If you are kind and friendly to everyone, you won't have to pick and choose. You'll be liked and respected by more people and those with less friends will think you are wonderful. The more I've been considerate and shown attention to people who didn't have a lot of friends or acceptance, the more I've been rewarded. Just think, going out of your way to be nice, to be kind to one who isn't liked or isn't cool doesn't cost you a thing. It develops loyalty that may reward you when you least expect it. You'll be appreciated and remembered because of your kindness to them because most people, if they aren't unfriendly to them, simply ignore them. You never know when that person may be in a position to do something to help you. I am reminded of the parable Jesus told his disciples. To paraphrase, he said, "Anytime you give a hungry man food, or a thirsty man water, you do these things for Me." Kindness and compassion are good traits to have, even in a sometimes ruthless business world. It helps you keep perspective. Recognize your team members' ideas, contributions and accomplishments. They will reward you with loyalty and hard work.

Encourage a Sense of Ownership

A sense of ownership can come in many forms. It can come from private ownership, owning stock in a company, or even from a feeling inside that you are an intricate part of a company. If you have a sense of ownership, you'll have a greater interest in seeing the company succeed. Your work won't be just a job, but an important part of the company.

We encourage our store managers to feel as if they are running their own little company. In some of our companies, we have established profit sharing, by setting aside a percentage of the profits to distribute to each employee. In our public companies, we offer stock options to those employees who have reached unit level management and above. Sharing ownership, by giving the employees the desire to see the income level rise, will make you more money in the long run.

Involvement in the Community Develops Pride

Encourage your team to be active in the community. The pride we develop for our community will carry over into the workplace. As we join civic and social organizations, we not only develop a sense of belonging, but we also learn about the inter-relationship between the community, our business, our own jobs in that business and our paychecks. We begin to see the vital role we each play in the progress of our community, and how the progress of our community affects our own individual progress.

Be active in the Chamber of Commerce. Be a volunteer board member of a charitable organization. Join a civic club that shares your interests. Run for public office as a school board member or city council member, or perhaps an even higher office.

There is a lady in the community I live in who was recently honored for her community service. She is the wife of a well-known university professor and has spent many years working with the United Way and the Red Cross. When she was given the honor, she very humbly replied, "Volunteering is the rent I pay for my time on this earth." This wonderful lady, Mrs. Jackie Wright, and her late husband, Dr. Ralph Wright, are outstanding examples of giving to others.

We need people in our businesses who have more purpose in their lives than just doing a job. We need people who know the sanctity of family and of service. It is these kinds of people who are capable of having vision and seeing a bigger picture than what is in front of them. They are leaders and visionaries, and we should be proud to have them working on our team.

Keep Employees Safe and Comfortable

Another concern of your employees is safe and comfortable working conditions. Businesses should furnish a break room, a first-aid station and proper levels of heating and cooling that will make the conditions comfortable. Businesses should encourage workers to take proper breaks. Managers should pay attention to employees' needs in the workplace.

If you have a department that is heavily computerized, you should provide the kind of lighting that is easy on the eyes. Those employees who have to do repeated physical movements, such as typing, stapling, or working with their hands should be made as comfortable as possible to avoid carpal tunnel.

Employers and managers should be well-educated on OSHA requirements and take precautions to safeguard their employees. Our employees should be well-trained in workplace safety. They should know how to avoid injuries.

If employees are safe and comfortable, they will be more efficient and productive with their time on the job. They will know their employer is concerned about their safety and well-being, thus motivating them further to do a good job.

Make Work Fun

When I was in school, I didn't like working in a grocery store. I used to work with my brother stocking shelves and carrying out groceries. These great big guys would come in and get their weekly groceries and I would carry them out in big boxes. I thought to myself, "That's okay, I don't need any help."

Even though I didn't necessarily enjoy this job, we made it tolerable by making it fun. We made it into a kind of game. According to Mary Poppins, "In every job that must be done, there is an element of fun." We would yell back and forth across the store. My brother usually called me Tex and I called him Lasso. We had nicknames for each other to make it fun. We'd yell back and forth and pretty soon the rest of the employees would get involved. The manager, a straight laced gentleman, Ted Edens, would just stand there, peering out under his bushy eyebrows. He didn't say a lot, but I think he saw what was happening; the enthusiasm level rose, workers got interested and started working harder. We worked from 8:00 a.m. until closing at 9:00 p.m. That was a thirteen hour day. THEN, we had to clean the store from top to bottom. If we didn't make the work fun, we wouldn't have been as nice to the customers. Howard, Bill and I, all brothers, were as different as night and day but we loved each other.

You need to make work as much fun as possible. I don't mean fun and games, I mean just fun. Every Friday at our offices, we have dress-down day. Sometimes we all bring a covered dish and have lunch together or order food delivered. We can look forward to Friday, because it makes the day a little bit easier and more comfortable. This summer we are experimenting with dressing down every day since Fridays worked so well. The only problem so far is defining what "dress down" is.

A friendly atmosphere makes work fun. Speaking to employees, inquiring about their families, talking to them about their vacations; all these things promote a fun workplace. Friendliness must be sincere, however. False friendliness will be seen quickly for what it is and can just as quickly lead the team in the other direction.

Heroes come in different fashions and personalities. It's the same in business. Heroes are often surprising. Take the time to get to know everyone you work with. You may learn amazing things from people you thought you knew. It takes very little to turn on ambitious, hard-working people. If you can gain their loyalty and motivate them, you are a leader.

Manage By Example

A wise person once said, "If the top man is no good, all the people below him will be no good in the same way." Our behavior is modeled by our superiors because we try to learn from them. This is important to understand, no matter which side you are on. As subordinates, we must be aware of who we choose to imitate. Choose good role models. As superiors, we must be aware that our subordinates will do as we do. They will not only pick up on our good habits, they will pick up on our bad ones as well.

If we find in our businesses a manager that has unacceptable behavior patterns, we know that behavior will be multiplied by the number of individuals under that manager. If a manager, for instance, has a too-relaxed approach to his job, perhaps taking his daily paperwork out to the front of the store and lounging there with a cup of coffee and a cigarette, then we've learned that the next person in charge will create the same overly-relaxed atmosphere. If you act in an appalling or obnoxious way to your customers, your subordinates will think it is okay for them to do the same thing when you are not there. As you do, so do your subordinates. If smoking and drinking is okay for the manager, then when the assistant manager or shift leader is there, in charge, they can do it too. That's what management privileges are, right??

Criticism Should Always be Constructive

It's unfortunate that most people can't take criticism, because that is how we learn and grow. Always say something positive first. If you are going to reprimand someone, take them aside and make a favorable comment first. Let them know they are doing some good things. Then explain your reprimand and why. If you give the employees the feeling that all you do is criticize them, then you leave a negative impact. Negativity breeds negativity.

I once knew an employer who only talked to his employees when he had a complaint with the job they were doing. They never heard positive comments. However, if he had something to complain about or criticize he was all over everyone. His favorite expression was (to be kinder than he) "Doodoo runs downhill." What he meant by that was if someone complained to him, he was going to pass down that criticism off his shoulders to everyone else.

The fact is, he was right. Doodoo does indeed run downhill. If the guy at the top isn't doing a good job, or has a negative personality, his employees most likely will be just like him. Emulation is commonplace in the workplace. If a person with poor work habits and behavior can be promoted or achieve a high position, his subordinates may think acting that way will get them promoted.

Allow Our Employees to Make Mistakes

I'm not going to allow my children to get hurt if I can avoid the pain for them. I'm going to try to teach them what I can and encourage them to consider all alternatives. But, I can't make decisions for them. I don't want them to do something just because I say so. I'd like to give them advice (but they never listen to that). I've been through pain, and I'd like to share some of my bad decisions along with my good ones, so they can learn from them. I can tell my children about those bad decisions and tell them what to watch for, but they have to make mistakes themselves before they will really believe it.

So it is with our employees. They have to take their swings at the plate. We all strike out occasionally; but if you don't step up to the plate and swing the bat, you'll never know. I encourage managers and supervisors in the organization to make their own decisions. You should review your concerns with the employee before he acts, but ultimately, you must let the employee make their own mistakes and successes.

You can give them advice, but in the end, let it be their call. Sometimes, you will know they are heading right into a mistake. However, those employees who have the courage to try to make a decision they believe is in the best interest of the company-right or wrong-deserve your support. If they make a mistake, you can only hope they learn from it.

Good judgment is the ability to balance pros and cons and make good decisions. Practicality is when you can admit you were wrong.

Support the Team

A well-tuned, well-run organization will rarely hit a bump along the road to success. If time and effort has been spent in building the right team and keeping the right people in place, then things should go smoothly. Occasionally, circumstances beyond our control, and sometimes within our control, do cause things to go off course. After all, people are people, and we all make mistakes. We all have imperfections.

It's important to support the concept of the team. Individuals on the team should support and encourage one another. If they cannot, then something may have to be done to protect the integrity of the team. Not only must supervisors and managers share the credit, workers must share credit among themselves.

If, as a business owner, manager or supervisor, you can build a good team work ethic and show concern and support for those people under your supervision, the team will carry on and persevere, even in times of crisis.

An occasional bump or crisis will be handled smoothly and the ship will stay on course. Developing this kind of teamwork takes a great deal of time, effort, blood, sweat and tears-in other words, total commitment on the part of the owner, manager or supervisor. If your subordinates have had an opportunity to get to know you and trust you, they'll work harder for you.

Stay in the Picture

It is important to say right now that as you build your company and organization, and as the corporate structure forms, you as entrepreneur and owner must stay in the picture. Once you begin to construct levels of management, you must carefully safeguard your own role in running the operation.

If we are in battle (and I believe business is like a battle) then to win we must make personal sacrifice. That's where the action is, standing shoulder to shoulder beside your troops in battle. You must be a cohesive, synchronized unit to function perfectly. Each must rely on the others to be there and to protect their area of responsibility. Without individual support from every flank, you have the possibility of a weakened segment. This vulnerability can be minor, or dangerous or devastating. You can lead people into battle. You cannot be effective by commanding them into battle. Battles are won by over-achievers. Success is won by over-achievers. Natural talent wins a lot, but the best champions are over-achievers. Mental toughness and over-achievers are the traits of good TEAMS.

Your team needs continual strengthening, training and support. Your role is vital. You should give a sense of importance to day-to-day operations. Don't overestimate your importance, but don't underestimate it either! People dedicated to their role and not the organizational structure create success.

The closer you are to your customer, the more opportunity you will have to act quickly to customer demands. If you are in contact with what I call the firing line (where your company or personnel meet the customer), you will know how to set the right policies. You'll be prepared to call the right move and stay in touch with the marketplace. You can lose a lot of customers before you find out why if you are too far removed from the firing line.

Don't stay in your corporate office, micro-managing with graphs and charts. Stay in constant contact with your personnel and your customers! Be persistent in follow-up and consistent in follow through. Only expect what you inspect.

Taking small, well-planned steps in your management approach and keeping in contact with your personnel and customers will get you a lot further than simply following the latest management theory.

<u>Stay in the picture.</u>

Loyalty Works Both Ways

Where is your loyalty? Are you committed and loyal to the people who pay your salary? (Bosses, customers, taxpayers). Remember, if you can't be loyal to the payer of your salary, where is your head? Regardless of your opinion, this allegiance is deserved. (Those who are unloyal and critical of their employers tempt having a higher death rate.)

As you should be loyal to your employer, you should also consider being loyal to your employee. You should always keep foremost in your thoughts a way to give praise and recognition to every person you possibly can. It doesn't hurt to exaggerate a little while you're complimenting them. This praise, which must be sincere, will get results like better attitudes, more effort and desire, higher productivity and improved work quality.

Praise and appreciation helps people have self-confidence. People enjoy knowing they are appreciated and that their supervisors recognize them for doing something well. Their self-esteem will rise and their personal pride and assurance that they are capable will drive them toward excellence. The sound of their name being spoken or seeing it written is a signal to their "well being and pride." Hearing or seeing their recognition will build morale and make them go above and beyond your expectations.

Being recognized is the purest form of personal satisfaction and pride. It allows a feeling of importance and exposure to others that gives them the "moment of glory" we all need in our lives.

Many criminals or those who break the laws or the rules or behave badly are only looking for recognition in some form.

They are doing it the wrong way, but it is the only way they know to be noticed or to vent their frustrations or disregard for being a "nobody."

4
Living With The Reality of Change

People react to change in many different ways. It's normal for people to feel a little concerned about the effects of change and what it means for them and their livelihood. After all, most of us prefer to operate in some kind of comfort zone. People go through many different emotions when they are forced to accept change.

We've all had to cope with change. The death of a loved one. The reorganization of the company for which we work. The employment of a new supervisor. Change is a way of life, but it is still hard on us to accept the changes in our lives. Any time change occurs, we experience various emotions..some positive, some negative. Moving into new geography or school or workplace can be devastating to children, adults or families.

As a supervisor or leader in creating change for employees, it is important to understand how employees look at change and how it affects them. It is imperative that the leader guide employees through the rough times and make them ready and willing to perform the new tasks and responsibilities that will be required of them. To do this requires the leader to be positive, compassionate, team-oriented and especially adept at people skills.

The Seven Wonders of Change

Blanchard Training and Development, Inc., a company that provides management training, has identified several levels of change and emotions employees go through. People typically go through what is known as the seven "wonders" of change.

1. I WONDER if I'll ever get used to the new way.
   Do they know what they are doing?
   Are they qualified to make this decision?
   Will I be able to get comfortable with this?
2. I WONDER how I'll get along without_____.
   I have used or relied on that person or that piece of equipment.
3. I WONDER why I'm the only one in this mess.
   We feel isolated and indulge in our own little pity party.
4. I WONDER when they'll stop changing the rules on me.
5. I WONDER if I'll ever catch up.
6. I WONDER where I'll ever find what I need.
7. I WONDER what that was all about.
   We are afraid to ask if we don't understand what they are trying to tell us or what they expect of us.

When we get used to doing anything it's because we've gone through a learning curve and gotten comfortable with our knowledge and ability to "do the job", "procedure", "task". It's only natural that a disruption of our routine will lead to some discomfort.

If we have to learn all over again or do something different, we are forced to expend extra effort or we develop doubts and fears. When we are good or proficient at what we do and have expertise and capability we hate to disrupt our methodology. Change and improvement requires flexibility. Status quo leaves you behind eventually.

Will I Get Used to the New Way?

That is a question most asked by employees who are expecting the arrival of a new boss. It's a question asked by many employees whose companies are going through reorganization. Change makes people feel ill-at-ease and self-conscious. They'll feel like they are on display. They'll be cautious, perhaps a little paranoid.

As you factor in causing a change or reorganization at a company, it's important to understand these feelings. If you are coming in as a new supervisor, your subordinates are going to have many questions about how you do things.

Be honest and up-front with the employees. Tell them change is going to occur but that you are seeking their input and their ideas. Try to lay out your expectations in a way that will make them feel at ease. Assure them that you, too, are going through change as well, because you have a whole new team to direct. Let them know you are all in this together and that together you will work toward making the "new way" work out for everyone concerned.

People Will Think About What They Have to Give Up

When change occurs, a certain mourning process also occurs. After all, if people are used to having certain things or doing things a certain way, it is hard to give that up. People become dependent on routine to some extent. Regimentation develops a comfort in knowing that an acceptable procedure is working. This is especially true for those insecure individuals who lack the ability to be creative. Even secure creative people will fear the results of something different. If the routine is changed or taken away, they will legitimately mourn that loss.

As a new leader, you must acknowledge the losses and allow the employees to mourn. Be supportive and understanding. You may have to explain again and again why the change is necessary. In time, begin to lead the employees in focusing on the positive aspects of the change. After awhile, the new way will become the old way.

People Will Feel Alone

It's natural for employees to feel isolated and alone, as if the change affects them and only them. You, as the leader, must structure activities that create team involvement. Set up a support structure for the employees to help each other make it through the changes they are confronting.

Have frequent staff meetings and get ideas from the team about how to best accommodate the changes that are coming. Explain that it will take everyone's effort to make the changes occur.

People Can Handle Only So Much Change

Sometimes when a company reorganizes or a new supervisor or CEO comes on board, too much change is thrown at the employees. New management tries new things that may not work out, then they switch gears and change the rules again. It becomes very frustrating to the employees who are trying to cope and adapt.

A good management strategy is to set priorities for change and think long-term. Not all change will happen automatically or overnight. It is demoralizing to the team to constantly be deluged with change.

Plan a strategy, set the top priorities and work through each priority systematically. Ease the departments into change. Thoroughly think through how change will affect the business. Don't just try the latest new management strategy. Have a plan, work the plan carefully and keep your eye on the long-term picture.

People Are at Different Readiness Levels For Change

Businesses employ different kinds of people at every level. Some employees are risk-takers and willing to make changes; others are more comfort driven and less secure. Acknowledge this in the beginning and don't be too hard on those employees who may be less ready for change.

Get to know the people who are working with you. Take some time to talk to them, individually, to get an idea about how they feel about their jobs. Let those who seem eager and willing take the brunt of the changes first. Ease the others into change as much as possible. It will take more effort, but explore ways in which to bring those less secure employees into the idea stages. Create opportunities for these employees when they rise to the occasion. Be sincere in letting them know you appreciate their efforts.

People Will Be Concerned
They Don't Have Enough Resources
(time, money, skills, etc.)

Some employees may feel insecure about new responsibilities and tasks that are being required of them. In this time of corporate and industrial downsizing, fewer people are being required to take on more and more responsibilities.

Teamwork and creative problem solving really come in handy here. If all the employees know they are part of a team, you as coach and leader must make them understand that they have each other for support. Creative problem solving through team problem solving can help resolve some of these issues. Let the employees know you expect them to work with each other and together to make things happen. Where one employee may feel less secure in a skill, the others must use their skills to help and to teach.

It is important to note here that just because one team member may feel less secure in his skills, it doesn't mean it is appropriate to let that employee slack off and not do his share of the workload. If a team has one or two slackers and the others are making it up, that creates a morale problem.

A good coach will not tolerate a slacker and will take immediate steps to end that kind of behavior if he sees it coming. If he doesn't, the team could begin to lose cohesiveness and motivation and the leader risks losing credibility.

If You Take the Pressure Off, People Will Revert to Their Old Behaviors

The leader must maintain the focus of the change and continue to <u>manage the journey</u> through the change. Be positive minded and understanding with employee fears and concerns, but also be firm in focusing on the change that needs to take place.

People and Leadership Skills Required

Nothing is quite so challenging to a business owner or supervisor than leading a group of people into change. It's harder than starting a new team from scratch. It requires a leader who possesses an exceptional blend of management and people skills. There's not much room for learning in this kind of situation. Any kind of misstep could set a leader back several paces.

Keep in mind that both directive behavior and supportive behavior are required to help the employees and the leader through the change process.

Keeping a few rules in mind will help.

1. Tell employees what you expect of them. Tell them what to do, how to do it, where to do it and when to do it.
2. Set goals and make those goals clear. Show them what kind of results you expect.
3. Give them the opportunity to do the job.
4. Be there to support, correct and give feedback as needed.
5. Praise the progress they make. Don't wait for perfection. Remember, change takes time. Acknowledge the small s teps and praise anything you can.
6. Redirect. If you're not seeing the progress you expect, redirect their activities immediately. Give them feedback. Don't wait to see if the problem corrects itself. Take the lead in redirecting the employees where you want them to go.

5
Tolerance - a Necessity

When interaction with a large number of different people is in your daily activities, you will find it more and more necessary to develop your tolerance level. Expectations are always higher than results it seems, especially if you are setting the standards. If you have a grid or a standard measure, you better have your tolerances worked in.

My work experiences while I was growing up and getting my education are remembered as times when you were expected to be at your work station, with your tools and ready to be productive as soon as the clock struck starting time. You didn't stop and visit or talk idle talk while you were being paid. If there was a break, and there seldom was, you took the exact time allowed and no more. Lunch times and quitting times were exact and not "fudged on". The days before and after holidays were full days and not cut short. Eight hours work for eight hours pay. Nothing more, nothing less.

When I worked construction as a young man, if it was shoveling, the first shovelful took place at the appointed starting time of work. If it was carpentry, we had wood in place, nails in the nail bag, hammer in hand and first nail driven at starting time.

Today, people show up at starting time, have their gossip and conversation, get their coffee and finally get started opening their work day materials about twenty minutes later and become productive about half past the hour. The day before holidays everyone wants to leave early to prepare for it and take the next day off if it is a Friday.

The work place has become a social place. The social environment of the workplace today is the release from stress at home in two-income families. We can tolerate this as long as productivity levels meet our guidelines and allow us to operate in our necessary financial sphere.

Tolerance makes the workplace function, the family and marriages survive, children become reared properly and reach maturity. However, we must not be so tolerant that we lower our own standards too much.

We naturally become more tolerant as we get older. We are tougher on our first child than the second and third and so forth. We also become more tolerant by being "beaten down." We give in because we get tired of fighting. It gets easier to give in to the pressure than to stand our ground. We rationalize, procrastinate, worry about whether we are totally right and generally want to avoid as much conflict as possible. Where does this lead us? Right where the work place is today! More relaxed, a less productive work place. Of course innovation and technology have created many replacements for workers through automation and manpower has been replaced by machine power such as robots and mechanical production lines. Time and management studies have shown ways to improve efficiency and productivity. In the process, tolerance for today's work environment have been worked into our way of conducting our business. Even though it is very difficult, when you are old enough to have lived by the old standards, we have to accept the changes. Productivity has changed, benefits and wages have changed and tolerance levels have changed.

The governments have made it tougher and tougher to be in business. It's more expensive and often less profitable. We jump through hoops, butt our heads against the bureaucratic wall and wait for the next shoe to drop. Then after the battle with income and other taxes, we pay capital gains tax when we sell our business or part of it, and then if there is anything left when we die they charge us death taxes.

In spite of all this, I think the USA is the greatest country on earth, but tax wise we are a little out of hand.

PART V

A BUSINESS OF OF YOUR OWN

1
The Making of an Entrepreneur

The Entrepreneur's Credo

I do not choose to be a common man,
It is my right to be uncommon—if I can.
I see opportunity—not security.
I do not wish to be a kept citizen, humbled
and dulled by having the state look after me.

I want to take the calculated risk;
to dream and build,
to fail and to succeed.
I refuse to barter incentive for a dole.
I prefer the challenges of life
to the guaranteed existence;
the thrill of fulfillment to the stale calm of Utopia.

I will not trade freedom for beneficence
nor my dignity for a handout.
I will never cower before any master
nor bend to any threat,
It is my heritage to stand erect,
proud and unafraid;

giving of my time and money,
requiring both to qualify.
If I give only time,
I am an employee.
If I give only money,
I am an investor.
I must think and act for myself,
to enjoy the benefit of my creations
and to face the world boldly and say;
This with God's help, I have done.
All this is what it means to be an Entrepreneur.

This poem was written for the most part by someone else, I've no idea who, but I like it! An entrepreneur is a special person. Anyone who is willing to take a dream into reality is an entrepreneur. She has a desire for responsibility. She has a preference for moderate risk. She has confidence in her personal success, and she is a positive thinker.

Not everyone can be an entrepreneur, and that's not a put-down. The great thing about our country is that it needs all kinds of people to make our businesses run effectively. We need administrators, administrative assistants, technicians, researchers, etc. We need all these people, and not all of them are entrepreneurs, some are managers.

Entrepreneurs take risks, and that's what makes them special. Only those who take risks truly understand what risk is. I have found through the years that going into business with someone who has no financial investment (no risk) is usually never as effective as going into business with someone who does have financial investment.

It's pretty lonely at the top when the buck can't go beyond you, when the decision has to stop at your level and there is no place else for it to fall back to. When the company needs money and there is no one else to put the money up but you, then you face the burden of where you are going to get it. Is it available? What will the bankers say? Where is the additional capital going to come from?

This scenario happened to me a short time ago. One of our companies, that we had invested tons of money in, dropped a bombshell when they said, "We have to have this much money to survive the next 30 days." Because of the banking situation and conditions in the world today, it was a tremendous challenge. It was a situation where I truthfully did not know if I could come up with the needed funds. It puts you under a tremendous amount of stress. It takes a certain kind of person to deal with these kinds of situations. It takes a real entrepreneur.

Real entrepreneurs have several definitive characteristics.

**Real entrepreneurs** stay focused on the job to be done. They will do any job needed to make the project work, regardless of their job description. They are able to see the whole picture. They know they have to fit into the scheme of things.

**Real entrepreneurs** work underground as long as they can. They don't go around saying, "Look, I did something extra that wasn't even my job." They know that when they deserve recognition, they'll get it. They may have to work a little harder than everyone else. They may not get immediate recognition for it, but sooner or later, their accomplishments will become self-evident.

**Real entrepreneurs** never bet on a race unless they're running in it. They don't want their success to be dependent on anyone else.

Real entrepreneurs are true to their goals and realistic about the way to achieve them.

Real entrepreneurs preserve a desire to learn and improve at all stages of their career. The day you quit learning is the day you start slipping backward.

Real entrepreneurs are never satisfied. They are always searching for a better way and are always challenging themselves.

Real entrepreneurs associate with people like them - people who are on the rise. They work only with the best. They don't get pulled down by those who are going down. They associate with people who are enthusiastic, energetic people, people like them who care about their futures.

Real entrepreneurs develop centers of influence. They find people who have their interests at heart and want to see them succeed. Then, they follow their intuition about these people.

Real entrepreneurs always want to be a part of solving problems with answers. A loser is always a part of the problem.

Real entrepreneurs honor the people who sponsor them, those who are willing to take a fundamental risk on them. They never begrudge what their sponsors get in rewards.

Entrepreneurs built this country, and the entrepreneurial spirit still thrives today. Not all successful business people are entrepreneurs and not all entrepreneurs are successful business people. Many entrepreneurs out there are not successful......yet. They live with a dream and a goal of someday making it big. Entrepreneurs who don't let failure sway them will become successful.

All entrepreneurs have intuition, a sense of urgency about their work and their life. If you want to be an entrepreneur you must have a high energy level. You must be a self-starter. You must be able to get up in the morning, kick yourself in the bottom and get out there and get the job, whatever it might be, done. If you have all these qualities...you just might be an entrepreneur.

2
Picture Your Business

Many people dream of owning their own business. They are motivated by a number of things-money, management over their time, building their community. While many people have this dream, it is amazing how few people know how to make the dream a reality.

Starting a business is like building a house; you work from the ground up and the first thing you must have is a good foundation. The foundation of a business begins with a business plan.

The business plan is a snapshot of your business and how you intend to conduct it. This snapshot has five essential parts. First, you must have an idea of the service or product you want to provide. Second, you must have a plan to create sales of your product or service. Third you must know what kind of personnel you will need. Fourth, you need to know what kind of physical facilities you'll need and, last but certainly not least, you must know how you will finance your business. Distinguish between capital investment and operating capital.

Number One: It All Starts With a Good Idea!

To come up with that good idea for a business, you have to be creative and optimistic. Be alert. <u>Train yourself to look for ways of improving products and services</u>. <u>Be aware of people's interests and likes</u>. Most importantly, be aware of change. Our society is constantly changing, and <u>each change provides a wealth of opportunity</u>! Continually ask yourself, "Is there a better way to do this?" or, "How could this product work better?" It may be a service or product you could improve. It doesn't have to be exotic or new; there are simple opportunities everywhere. For example, as I'm sitting in my office, I might turn on a lamp. If I have trained myself to always be looking for improvement, I may notice that the lamp doesn't throw off good light and I'm going to start considering ways to improve that lamp.

Throughout the day, difficulties may arise with common everyday tasks. Once again, a trained mind begins looking for an easier, more efficient way. Perhaps you will find a better way to brush your teeth, prepare a meal or even shine your shoes. How many times do you suppose someone looked for their eyeglasses before they came up with the idea of putting a chain on them so they can hang around their neck? If it's a common situation, then many people could gain from your solution, and more importantly, pay for it.

Train yourself to review current businesses and services for improvements. Someone came up with the idea for a pizza. I'm told, contrary to popular belief, that pizza originated in the United States. Look at all the different types of restaurants and food items. There is always room for another kind of food.

Be aware of people's interests. Look for novelty items that

may interest people. The Chia Pet, a popular novelty item, is simply a way to grow grass in different shapes. What about the pet rock craze of a few years ago? Figurines of sport figures, celebrity likenesses, autographs, replicas of uniforms or wearing apparel are all huge businesses. A ballcap without a bill might be in line since so many young people are wearing their ball caps backwards!. The opportunities are limitless. You can find it where things are changing, (remember intuition?) and things are always changing.

Investment opportunities that look the least promising are often where real opportunities exist. This is particularly true in retail and service industries. Wal-Mart and other big discount houses sometimes seem unbeatable to small-town rural stores. But, the big discount centers do have weaknesses. They lack the personal service and a thorough knowledge of their products. And, they are usually crowded. Small businesses must seek ways to capitalize on those weaknesses in order to compete and be profitable. I have a friend who purchases her favorite perfume from a small retailer. Just before a business trip, she realized she didn't have enough to get her through the trip. When she went to purchase a refill, the small retailer hadn't been able to get any from the manufacturer and gave my friend her tester bottle to take on the trip. She just asked her to return what was left when she got back. No charge! That's the kind of extra service that a larger department or discount store simply can't and won't provide.

Trends and fashions keep changing. Once upon a time, people only wore lace-up shoes. A smart entrepreneur foresaw the fashion change and made a bundle off slip-on shoes. Who would have believed, back in the 1950's, that people in the

'90's would be wearing undershirts as outerwear? Now the T-shirt industry is enormous. In the restaurant business, someone came up with the salad bar and the buffet line. Just 20 years ago, only full-service cafeterias offered those items. Now, almost everyone offers a buffet line or all-you-can eat bar. Watch how things are changing and find ways to capitalize on that change.

Opportunities exist in technologies and business that are just getting off the ground. When I got into the Pizza Hut business, I found that a lot of the people had no more experience with pizza than I did. As a matter of fact, many people had never tried pizza in the communities where we were developing Pizza Huts. We became pioneers, so to speak. Sometimes when you are pioneering and breaking ground, you can get into a business that you could not otherwise afford to get into.

Know The Business You Intend To Start
Do Your Homework!

An important factor in coming up with a business idea is that you should know something about that business before you start. Never start a business you know nothing about!

Acquire all the knowledge you can about a business. Never work on preconceived ideas. Most of the time they will prove to be false. Do your homework. Study a similar business. You have to do research and analysis. You need to find out where the market place is. Is it a thriving community, is it a blue collar community, low income, high income? These are all crucial questions you need to research and analyze.

Know who your customers will be and your potential share of those customers. Is your market on premise or off premise?

You have to look beyond your own world to find those answers.

Before going into the plastic business, I went around the country visiting plants that manufactured plastic bags. Some let me see their plants, some didn't, but I learned from the conversations. Next, I went to different equipment manufacturers and tried to learn about equipment. In selecting equipment we made some deals which were poor choices and that made our job harder and more difficult. Thanks to the expertise of people like Ron Black and Craig Currier, we survived and have done well.

When Pitt Plastics first went into business, we relied heavily on one person's knowledge of how to manufacture plastic bags. We hired a plant manager even before we had finished construction of the plant. We sent him to another plant in Ohio to train for six months. We were depending solely on the expertise this one man was accumulating. This was a dangerous position to put ourselves in. And sure enough, a crisis developed. Marv Ackerson had learned well and developed the knowledge and expertise we needed. Unfortunately for him and us, just before we were to begin production, our plastics expert was in a very serious automobile accident. Another car ran him off the road into a bridge railing. He ended up with 13 feet of three-inch pipe through his lower abdomen and him. His sciatic nerve was damaged and it was uncertain whether or not he would survive. After a few days of worry and vigilance, we were relieved to learn that he would pull through. Today he is strong and healthy, he has a slight limp, but can fall off roofs onto concrete and only get bruised. Marv is a fighter and would have been a tremendous asset to our company.

In this time of crisis, we all pulled together and learned how to operate the plant, but it took us a long time to produce our first plastic bag. We learned a valuable lesson. It is important to have know-how and depth in your business. Don't rely too much on the knowledge of others and never have only one individual with all the key knowledge.

Second: Have A Plan To Generate Sales

Okay, now you know what kind of business you want to start. How are you going to get people to buy your service or product? There are three phases to generating sales: Marketing, Advertising and Quality (and service).

Marketing consists of identifying who your potential customers might be and then devising a plan to get those customers to buy your product or service (or come to your store).

There are a number of ways to identify potential customers. You need to do some research on the age group, gender, financial status and other identifying factors of your target market. You need to know the number of potential customers to determine how lucrative your business might be.

For example, at National Mills, we produce thousands of dozens of T-shirts a week. That's a lot of T-shirts isn't it? But guess what? We only have to produce a very small percent of the T-shirt industry in order to be successful. We have to have less than 2% of the entire industry because this industry is a billion upon billion dollar business.

Your marketing must determine the spread as to where your sales will come from. The broader your market and the less market share you need the greater your chance of having a profitable business.

Marketing is an art, not a science. Just because you do this research and devise a plan one time doesn't mean it will be valid forever. As I have said many times before and will say many times again, things change. The best thing you can hope for is to beat the percentages. The way you beat the percentages is by trying lots of different things in different ways. Many people in marketing research will disagree with me on this. They'll say, "We can tell you if you do this and you do that it's going to work." But demographics change constantly. People's emotions change. New inventions bring change in demand of products (intuition again). Be on the lookout for new ideas in marketing your products and keep tabs on your customers' needs. The best marketing tool is a good (hopefully outstanding) product or service. If your customers thoroughly enjoy your product or service and are happy with it, they'll tell their friends and word of mouth takes over.

In addition to all of this, once you have identified your target market, you must devise a plan to get those people to buy your product. You have to find a way to let people know your product or service exists. You need to advertise.

Many people fail to see the importance of advertising. Actually, we know only 50% of all advertising works. The only difficulty is that we don't know which 50% of the total 100% is the part that works. Therefore, we can't eliminate any of the program without taking a chance of destroying its effectiveness. In fact, when businesses are in trouble, they often cut their advertising budget, thinking that it is a luxury. Advertising is a necessity, and it doesn't have to be expensive.

Most people equate advertising with only one medium...television. Television is the most expensive form of advertising and the best way to reach the masses. Most small businesses don't need to reach the masses! They need to reach a smaller target market. Today, even television comes in so many forms that the forms that can afford to use it must approach it in a broader spectrum.

Advertising may be as simple as putting a sign in front of your business. Advertising may involve telemarketing, calling your potential customers. It may be using a direct mail piece. Your business may be the kind that could benefit from advertising in the yellow pages of your local phone book.

You can find a number of ways to get exposure for your business. Get involved in your local Chamber of Commerce. Attend Chamber events and get to know those people. Find ways to promote your business through Chamber services— hosting a coffee or reception at your business or attending a trade show. Even large firms or businesses should do the same thing on a local basis in every community they are in. If you are a good corporate community citizen, your customers will feel good about doing business with you.

Once you build a customer base and your customers have an idea of the quality and reliability of your service or product, word-of-mouth advertising will take place. That's why I put the third factor in the formula for generating sales...quality and along with it, customer service.

It doesn't matter how much money you spend on marketing and advertising, if you don't have a quality product, sales will not happen. You might get Sale Number One, but if your product is no good, you won't have repeat business. It is hard to get the customer the first time. If you get that first customer and fail to impress him with your quality and service, it's darn near impossible to get him back and you can be sure you won't get any of his friends either!

That's why customer service is so critical. Anyone can walk into any big discount house and buy furniture, a major appliance, window coverings, you name it. The big discount houses can offer these products at a lower price because they can buy in volume. But what happens if the product breaks, or doesn't work properly? Who will make it right? They may replace the product, but what about the labor involved in re-installation and time wasted trying to find the problem?

Companies who specialize in certain products and, therefore may have to offer them at a higher price than the discount houses, must be able to sell the consumer on their product's quality and their customer service. If a consumer is not treated well by the business, he won't be back. Quality and service must be ingrained in your mind *and* in the minds of your employees from the get-go!

Pizza Hut is a good example of how a business can still dominate the market, even with a little higher price. When it comes to price, many other pizza places sell for less. The service in those other places is okay. But when it come to quality, many have shortcomings. Our ingredients are fresh and real. We don't use imitation anything! Our large pies are bigger than most other pizza places. We strive to provide the best service possible to our customers.

Have you ever considered what percentage of people don't complain? Ninety-six percent of the people who are dissatisfied with your product or service won't complain. Let's say you get one unsatisfactory comment card from one person, that means there are probably 96 other people sitting out there thinking the same thing!

As I said, getting sales is no easy task. It's rare that a business starts out and has an easy time of it. It happens occasionally, like a software company or computer company with a unique product that everyone wants (Windows '95). Or a new restaurant opens in a small town and everyone eats there, at least once. Maybe the restaurant will go gangbusters for awhile, but eventually, they have to find ways to remind their target market about their product or service.

Your plan on how to create sales should include some kind of budgeted amount you think it will take to do the necessary marketing and advertising. You should research the media you intend to use and include costs for advertising with that media.

It is important to analyze every promotion you run. Like I said before, you may have to try many different things to find the right approach to sales for your particular product or service. Don't be too discouraged if one of your "great ideas" for a promotion doesn't work. It may work at some later time. The secret is to communicate with your customers. Analyze and review each promotion from their perspective. Try to find out why the results were what they were, good or bad.

Third: Personnel and Training

What kind of people will be needed to operate your business? Are you the only employee? Do you have the necessary skills to produce the product or service? If you are not the only employee, how many employees will you need? What kind of skills will these other employees need to have? What will you have to pay them? What kind of benefits can you afford to provide for them? Does your service or product require a lot of training or re-training of personnel? How often will this re-training need to take place?

Once you have answered all these questions and hired your personnel, you should ask each worker to write out their understanding of their job description. They should include their job responsibilities and goals for the next 30, 60 and 90 days. Periodically go back and review these written goals to see if they are being accomplished. This will help show you their productivity levels and put the onus on them to judge and grade themselves. This will provide them with their own incentive and motivation to succeed instead of being driven by their supervisors. It should also include their philosophy and why it's important to them and why it's good for you. It should also include how productivity, profitability and a pleasant environment are important. It is our people skills and our own ability to interact and develop respect, admiration and loyalty that can make a difference. If we want loyalty we have to be loyal and compassionate. Respect, Dignity, Cordiality, Kindness, these are key words for any business.

Fourth: Physical Location

You've picked the business you want to pursue. You've hired your people. Where are you going to put them? One of the important factors to any business plan is the location of the actual facility and the physical requirements of your business. Let's assume your business requires a physical location outside your home.

You've got to find a location you can afford that will fit within the framework of your business. You must choose whether to build, rent or purchase a building. You must carefully consider the site on which you will locate your business. You must also consider what you can afford. Will your business require a lot of traffic? Do you need a large parking lot? What kind of handicapped accessibility will your particular business require?

These are all things that you must consider and think out before you actually go into business. Remember, that in some businesses, location is critical. So is zoning. You must be aware of your city's zoning laws. You should make contact with your city's building officials at the beginning of the project. Your building will be required to meet certain codes, so you need to know what those codes are and what kinds of cost will be incurred in meeting them.

You should also check to see if you qualify for any tax abatements, enterprise zone incentives or low-interest loans. Many cities have set aside funds to help businesses which meet certain economic development requirements.

Again, research, analysis, homework. These challenges need to be met and resolved **before** you ever open the doors for your business.

Fifth: Where Will You Get the Money?

We've put money as the fifth phase of the business plan, but it could really be considered the first. To start a business, you must have capital. If you don't have your own money, you'll have to find sources (investors) who are willing to put up the money .

It's a good idea to have your own money in your business. If you have to rely on too many investors, you could end up in a power struggle and find yourself completely out of the business that was your dream and creation. Remember the money you get from investors is a cost.

A few years ago I had an option to buy a major league baseball club. The cost of borrowing the money was 20-21%. I felt that was too much. Besides, the baseball club's corporate structure was sub-chapter S under the Revenue Codes, and that offered problems in paying for the investment. Sub-Chapter S corporations are taxed as individuals. This means that you pay taxes on earnings whether you take them out or not. In a regular corporation you pay corporate tax but you don't pay personal tax until you take funds out. It is double taxation if you take out some of your earnings from a regular corporation, but you can pay off debt or grow your company and only pay a smaller tax(corporate) instead of personal rates if you don't take any personal money out. Buying the baseball club would have been easier if it had been a regular corporation. If it costs too much to borrow the money, maybe you don't want to go into the business. The cost of the money may run all your profits out the back door. Your capital must be figured into the cost of operating your business and subtracted before profits are realized.

The most difficult thing in developing a company is getting the financing. Banks are unwilling to finance dreams or ideas. They only look at hard assets! My first loan was secured out of town because none of the local banks would make a loan to me.

One of the challenges is finding a way to start a business with as little investment as possible. Most likely, you will have to borrow some of the money to begin your business. Be assured, you will need a detailed, written business plan in order to borrow from a credible lender.

Lenders have certain guidelines they consider when they decide to loan or invest in a business. Below is a list of the characteristics of the ideal small business borrower:

1. Good capitalization or retained earnings in business.
2. Good management skills.
3. Knowledge and experience in business area.
4. Good character.
5. Good credit history.
6. Growth potential.
7. Good collateral.
8. Good planning and product.
9. Liquidity.
10. Personal equity invested in the business.

If you are already in business, but looking to expand or begin an offshoot business, you need to add the following to the above list:

11. Good profit history.
12. Good accounting methods and financial statements.
13. Increasing sales or market share.
14. Keeps lenders informed of status of business.

The major reasons for rejecting a small business loan application include:

1. Undercapitalization or too much debt.
2. Lack of collateral.
3. Inability to demonstrate source of repayment.
4. Poor credit history.
5. Inadequate financial information.
6. Weak management.
7. Applicant lacks experience in his field of business.
8. Poor track record or poor profitability.

9. Unprofessional financial statements.
10. Unreliable records.
11. Poor planning.
12. Bank services not used to full advantage.

There are a number of sources to help you with finding the financing for your business. You should contact the Small Business Administration for information. If you live near a university, you should check with them to see if they offer assistance to entrepreneurs looking to start a new business.

Look Ahead

There is another factor to your business snapshot. You must think about the long-range outlook for your business. It is a very methodical, logical, slow-moving process to build a business. Once you've managed to open your business, you must operate it conservatively and preserve funds.

Some people look at conservatism as miserly, but a miser is overly zealous and foolish about conservatism, hoarding money when it makes more sense to spend it. Being conservative isn't being miserly, it's being smart!

A conservative approach is something on which you must constantly work. You must train and retrain yourself to look for unnecessary spending. (Pay attention to "Termites" in the next chapter.)

Start small, keep spending down and keep reinvesting. As your business grows and you enjoy some success, don't lose focus of the bottom line. Remember, as times change, so could your business. Things happen quickly in today's economy, so be on guard.

I am reminded of the story of the Pony Express rider whose

horse gave out on him. He stopped at the farm of a minister who lived in the middle of nowhere. The rider asked the minister for a horse. After some negotiations, the minister gave the rider his only horse. The rider jumped on the horse and said, "Giddy up" but the horse didn't move. He said it again, and still the horse didn't move.

"You have to say 'Praise the Lord' to get him to go," explained the minister. "And, you have to say 'Amen' for him to stop."

So, the rider said, "Praise the Lord." Sure enough, the horse took off like a shot. The horse was running wildly, and it was all the rider could do to stay in the saddle. Suddenly he saw a cliff ahead of him, and in his terror, he couldn't remember what the minister told him to say to stop the horse.

"Whoa," the rider yelled. "WHOA! WHOA!" but the horse wouldn't stop.

Finally, the rider remembered to say, "AMEN," and the horse came to an abrupt halt right at the edge of the cliff. The rider leaned uneasily over and looked at the gaping hole below him. He leaned back in the saddle, took off his hat, dusted his brow and said, "Whew! Praise the Lord!"

Don't operate your business the way the Pony Express rider operated his horse!

See the Whole Picture

One other thing to keep in mind. John Tigrett is a man whom I admire greatly and listen to carefully when he says anything. His business expertise and knowledge came from doing business deals all over the world with some of the most famous business leaders of this century. He is a good friend and wise counsel of mine and once told me that if you have a business, store or investment that is not doing well and hasn't done well, and you don't see immediate improvement happening, then don't stay with it. Cut your losses, take your hit and go on.

If you do the type of planning I've outlined, you should be able to start your business and judge the success of it as you go along. You should see opportunity to eliminate your losses or provide additional profits.

Few people in the business world understand the whole spectrum of what business is and how to make a bottom line profitable. People get caught up in the glamour of doing a high sales volume. They don't realize that it doesn't matter how much you sell if you don't apply the money to the bottom line so you can pay off debts, increase the size of your business or give dividends and bonuses.

If you follow this general guideline in starting and running your business, success and accomplishment are only a matter of time. A few people and only a few have the ability to start and be successful in more than one business. Mr. Tigrett's son Isaac has done that. After starting Hard Rock Cafe and subsequently selling it he has now started The House of Blues, another success. Incidentally, he took his profits from the sale of Hard Rock Cafe and built a great humanitarian hospital in India. Isaac and his partners are true entrepreneurs.

Great Ideas, Big Dreams and Great Planning.

Create your dream or be a valuable part of a team!
That may be more simple than it seems
Since no I appears in team
It is I who will dream and find a team!
Success takes "all together" effort and can't be singular in nature.

3
Conservatism is the Key

In the preceding chapter we touched briefly on conservatism. It doesn't matter what your politics are, conservatism is a requirement for success in the business world. There are two very important things to do when you start a company:

1. *Keep bureaucracy out.*

2. *Keep your culture.*

When a business is starting out, any money your business makes needs to be reinvested back into the business. In the beginning, most of the profits should go to improvements and growth. Paying for the business loan and investments should supersede any personal profit. Expenses have to be controlled to a finite point so that you totally maximize profits. This is the mentality that keeps a business thriving.

Keep Bureaucracy Out

What happens to some businesses as they progress and expand is that they begin to bring in outside people...people with corporate backgrounds. Unfortunately, many corporate executives have lost, to a degree, their conservatism. By that I mean corporate dollars seem like Monopoly®, money to some people. If you are dealing in high sales and volume, then you get to a point where it doesn't bother you to spend another $10,000 or give somebody another bonus or to raise wages to where they are out of reason. Some corporate mentality is that if you are working for a corporation, that money is not the same as the money you spend at home. It is very easy for employees to order some kind of a trinket, a give-away or a promotional item, knowing that if they buy a bunch of jackets, caps, briefcases, pencils, paper, pads, pocket calendars or whatever, they get one too. Some people would rather spend the money to get an order of 2,000 items of something just so they can get one. They don't care about the corporate dollar, they simply want one of what they order.

I've had people say to me, "Why don't you invest in this?" I say, "I don't like it. It's not a good investment." Their reply is that I can always "write it off" my income tax. I scratch my head and say, "Income tax is 37-38%, and I'm still going to lose 62%. That doesn't make good sense to me."

I can write off everything I want. I've seen people write things off their taxes until they have to file bankruptcy. That is the wrong mentality in my mind.

If a vendor sells a product for 20 cents a pound more than another vendor, that may not seem like much of a difference. But, buy 1,000 pounds of that product and that little difference adds up. Sound management watches pennies in costs and keeps an eye on adequate quality.

In this area corporate mentality sometimes goes way off the mark. What happens when you allow spending or the allocation of funds to go to the extreme? What happens next year?

As an example, let's say a company has a good year and the executives decide to give everybody a big raise. Then the next year, things aren't so good and there is no money for any kind of raise. What does this do to employee morale? The bureaucracy, or corporate mentality, is that you give employees whatever you want to give them this year and don't worry about ten years down the road, or even next year.

Don't get me wrong. I'm not against rewarding employees. After all, it is to a company's advantage to pay competitive wages to their employees and provide competitive benefits. But the objective should be to keep that business afloat and keep those employees employed for many years to come. Companies must plan so that they keep their employees satisfied every year. If employees constantly expect some extra reward, one year without it will start a decline in effort or productivity. If you give some increase during a bad year, you can encourage employees with proper communication about how much their extra effort and input are needed.

I like the concept of profit sharing—giving incentives on the order of stock options or retirement plans. Helping our employees have a secure future is valuable and it contributes to an employee's longevity with your company.

Today's business owners have found it necessary to project twenty to thirty years down the road when hiring new employees. Businesses have to offer competitive wages, but they also have to be <u>wary of having employees who are overpriced for their jobs.</u>

Historically, that's happened to many of the bigger companies. Their executives reach the age of 45 to 50 and companies have to give them incentives (force them) to retire because they have gotten to such a high wage level that the work they are doing could actually be purchased at a much lower rate in today's marketplace.

The best way to bring competent and loyal executives into your business is to promote them from within. Of course, that means you need to look at every employee, from the mail room clerk to the secretary, as a potential executive in your company. People develop ambition and drive, and every time you promote from within, you send a signal to the other employees that you want to utilize those who have already committed to the company. Therefore, your goal should be to have a promotable person in every position in your company. *From the bottom up* should be your challenge. <u>The best employees are those who train their own replacement</u>.

Keep Your Culture

Culture, in this sense, is your method of operation. It is the way you conduct your business. Culture is a nature. Culture is being conservative or extravagant. It's training and retraining. It is keeping and developing long-tenured employees, thereby eliminating radical turnover. It is the way you handle your profits. It is the long-range planning of where you want to be tomorrow and 20 years down the road.

In good business practices, culture is the attitude of the company's operators in their approach to work habits. It is the every-day attitude in their approach to lower or upper management. Bad habits can also be a culture.

When you build your company from within by continually training and promoting your employees, you have a better chance of keeping your culture. Employees who have been with your company and have been a part of its growth are extremely valuable. Most often, they feel a sense of ownership and pride at what's been achieved. They must feel that they are a part of the success and achievements. These employees take the company's success very seriously. We depend on long-time employees to train our new employees and set an example of the kind of workplace we want.

At NPC International, we like to promote from within. We like to bring people up through the ranks and train them. We like to develop them so they are ready to be promoted to higher things. As I said earlier, I resist using employment agencies. I figure the people who are worth hiring are so busy doing their own jobs, they don't have time to go out and look for another one.

However, as I also said earlier, sometimes it is necessary to bring in individuals from the outside. This can be risky. The individual may have excellent business savvy. She may have all the abilities and qualifications required for the jobs. She may have past experiences that, on paper, would make her an ideal manager. Just keep in mind, if she will leave one company for you, she may leave you for another company. What you don't know is whether after you hire her, she can adjust to the way YOU do business. Can she adjust to your environment and philosophy? Can she adopt your conservative approach? These are tough questions. Remember, you could be stuck with a poor hiring choice until retirement...your retirement!

We grew through the 1960's and 70's and as we continued to get larger and generate more sales, in 1982 we decided to go public. After an 18-month process, we were able to go public in August, 1984.

With growth comes change. We now have a more structured management chain, from my position as Chairman of the

Board and Chief Executive Officer, to a President and Vice Presidents, Divisional Presidents with a supporting staff of marketing, human resources, development and chief financial officer. Along with these positions, we have a staff of office personnel-employees totaling over 17,000. We have offices in Dallas, Little Rock, Memphis, Southern Mississippi, Springfield, MO, and Birmingham. Our mid-management structure includes President of Operations to Regional Vice Presidents, Regional Managers to Area General Managers and individual unit Managers and Assistants.

In our manufacturing companies, we have a Board Chairman, President, Vice Presidents and support staff in human resources, marketing, brokerage and sales, as well as production superintendents, supervisors, trainers and shift leaders.

As an entrepreneur, I have found it difficult to cope with the amount of corporate bureaucracy that creeps into our companies. Through the process of growing and becoming a larger, yet still relatively small corporation, we have had a certain amount of this bureaucracy seep into our businesses. By corporate bureaucracy, I mean less control of our spendables; less control of our overall costs. It is a constant battle. The larger you get the less expendables are guarded and the more corporate money seems to become monopoly money to some. The larger you become the more difficult it is to keep your expenses at the level that you, as an entrepreneur and founder of the company, feel they should be. "Termites" start to creep in, and the larger the corporate bureaucracy, the harder it is to keep the termites out.

What are Termites?

The termite is a little bug that eats away at you...
He makes his way in hidden things and chews and chews and chews...
He makes his living eating those mistakes you may have caused...
You really can't restrain him 'cause he's just within the law....
The termites breed in springtime, when love is all about.
He also thrives in businesses, of that there is no doubt...
To kill him, you expose him, eject him from your mind.
Termite proof your memory, his death must be in time...
*You've killed the little ******, you really did him in.*
You've cleared your mind for thinking of the things that make you win...
You're sure to be successful, you've fought the battle bold.
You've termite-proofed your thinking before he got a hold...
The termite is a little bug that eats away at you,
You took away his diet and you killed this one, 'tis true.
But termites are big breeders, they're sure to produce their kind...
So be on guard for their return to the woodwork of your mind!

This is a simple and maybe silly little poem referring to little expenditures considered inconsequential or meaningless because they are considered small. But together they get into the walls of your business and become destructive. It describes an insect that each year people pay thousands of dollars to eradicate from their homes and businesses because it can be so destructive. We all know a termite can cause the demise of an entire structure.

Yet, what do we do about the termites that live in the framework of our businesses? Not our physical plants or buildings, but our whole sense of doing business?

Termites in your business can be a number of things. These termites create unnecessary overhead and costs. Additional management positions in the organizational chart is another area of which to be cautious. Poor time management is a termite.

A friend, who was running a repair business, came to me one time and asked, "Will you come out and talk to me? I'm running a business out here and I've got all the customers I can handle, but I'm not making any money."

Well, I went out and looked over his business. He was right. His yard was full of broken equipment that needed fixing. I observed him greeting customers as they brought him their broken items. He spent time with each of them as they left their equipment. And, he spent time with them again when they came in to retrieve it. He spent time on the telephone when it rang. He worked the cash register. What he didn't spend enough time doing was repairing the equipment. He was a one-man operation doing all the jobs in that operation. However, the only job that paid him any money was the actual repairs.

It didn't take more than ten minutes to pinpoint what I believed was his biggest termite, poor time management. I suggested he get some desk help to provide his customer service, like greeting his customers and answering the phone. He needed to use his expertise repairing the equipment. The cost of hiring some part-time help would be more than offset by the increase in repairs that he would be free to make. The lesson this gentlemen learned is that if you overvalue your strategy and undervalue the execution of running a business, it will lead to termites.

You have to keep control of your business, because if you don't it will control you. It is easy for someone else to say, "Why don't you rent this computer? It's only $300 a month."

Or, "Why don't you lease this car instead of that one? It's only $100 more." You have to exercise scrutiny over all costs.

When you run a large company with several levels of management, it becomes more difficult to control spending at all levels. That's why you have to train your managers and workers to understand from the beginning the importance of keeping expenses at a minimum and guard all costs. Every dollar you save goes right to the bottom line. Seems simple doesn't it? Common sense again, right? Why do I mention this, you knew it. It's as old and basic as time itself. Everyone knows how to be conservative. The reason is because you have to continually reinforce the philosophy. Not everyone has a financial stake. Since their money isn't invested, they aren't as motivated to watch for unnecessary expenses.

Many corporate employees get an irreverent attitude about corporate dollars. Statements such as, "Oh, it's only $1,000 or $5,000" projects the wrong attitude because every $1,000 and $5,000 add up. Twenty $5,000 savings add up to $100,000. It is as important to watch the $10 expenses when you're a $500 million company as it is when you are starting new with no sales. Single dollars lost are termites, whether they are noticed or not. Wasted unnecessary phone calls, overnight mail instead of regular mail when it's not a rush situation, non-productive employees...they're all termites that eat away at the bottom line profits of your business.

I had a meeting one morning with two of my executive committee members and there was a question about not having an expense account item approved. I had to ask one of them, "How does a subscription to <u>Sports Illustrated</u> help you in your job?"

Another company's president, whose company was losing money, couldn't understand why two dinners in Las Vegas, totaling $1,500, was rejected. Nor could he understand why a $500 mobile phone bill was rejected. It wasn't that these expenses may not have been justified or rationalized, it is just simple economics; when you are losing money, or starting out, you don't spend **any** money that can be saved. He couldn't understand that these types of expenses were a direct impact on the bottom line of the company he was running. All expense items must be scrutinized for termite control.

The founders and builders of any company, no matter how large, remember how tough it was in the beginning and the sacrifices it took to achieve success. They had to watch the "termites." They had to constantly put earnings back into the business, conserve, watch and save pennies. It took lots of hard work, long hours, total commitment and total account-ability to themselves and their creditors. They spent as little as possible in order to survive.

After you "make it," it is wise to never forget from whence you came. Never lose that feeling of being "poor." <u>I have never been motivated by the desire to get rich but rather driven by the fear of being poor</u>.

Many people go through life spending every penny they earn, never even thinking about saving or conserving. They expect someone else to provide for their emergencies, medical catastrophes and retirement. Saving for a rainy day, college or unexpected occurrences is everyone's obligation. It doesn't matter how much money you have or how much you think you are going to inherit. People who think they are rich today may find inflation or taxes destroying their ability to live comfortably later on in life.

The fallacy of expecting the government or your company to do it all for you is only going to cause disappointment. A good formula approach is to have social security, company (or work) and personal savings for a third each. Your home, pleasures and extras should be paid for during your working years.

Our People Must Understand Profit

Employees who work for companies come to their job each day, clock in, put in their hours doing their job, and then go home. As long as they do a good job, they depend on their employer to pay them their wage on schedule, provide them benefits and pay raises and to stay in business so they can keep going to work every day. These are not unreasonable expectations from our employees.

But, employers, also, should expect their employees to understand the meaning of company profit. This is why termite control is so important. In order for a company to be successful, every dollar and every expense must be watched. The financial health of a company should be common knowledge among employees. It is a good idea to hold training sessions focusing on company profits with employees at all levels. Employees should understand their cost to the company. They should understand that their salary, benefits, vacation, sick leave, social security, insurance, retirement, bonuses and other rewards are expenses. They should know what they take home isn't their only cost to the company.

We must constantly retrain our employees to think conservatively in their jobs, and to keep in mind that as the company grows and prospers, they have the opportunity to grow and prosper with it. But if employee spending and other "termites" get out of control, they put themselves and others at risk of not having a job to go to. Watch out for double standards. In other words, everyone else should exercise control of expenses, but not them. These people expect everyone else to watch the bottom line, but consider their expenses as okay. They don't really buy into conservatism or culture. They are too self-centered or selfish to give up anything.

Consider the following commandments to help you remember the true meaning of conservatism:

Ten Commandments of Conservatism

1. Thou shalt spend company funds as though they were thy own.
   (Would I spend it if it were my own money?)
2. Thou shalt insure that all costs are offset by their benefits.
   (Will the results be worth the cost?)
3. Thou shalt avoid extravagance.
   (Could it be done less expensively?)
4. Thou shalt seek to insure that for each dollar spent, earnings is thy reward.
   (Will it pay for itself?)
5. Thou shalt choose the optimal time to incur expenses.
   (Is this the most affordable time?)
6. Thou shalt choose alternatives with the highest return for thy investment.
   (Would it be less costly to do it another way?)
7. Thou shalt use the most efficient and effective method of communication.
   (Is a telephone call necessary or will a written note accomplish the task?)

8. Thou shalt plan all travel to minimize the cost and accomplish all goals.
(Make trips long enough to cover all areas of training and retraining and make all relevant calls on locations and customer base so as to minimize travel costs. Instead of traveling to Cleveland this week for two days and then have to go back to Ohio a week later, stay 4 days and catch Akron and its calls. This saves travel expenses and you still see all your customers.)
9. Thou shalt only request of others what thee would have requested of thyself.
(Don't ask anyone to do anything you wouldn't do or set a double standard for yourself. As we do, so do our subordinates.)
10. Thou shalt show termites unto others and they shalt show them unto you.
(Show the costs of car, motel, restaurants, tips, etc. Set acceptable charges and expenses for travel.)

Money Gets 80% of the Business

Getting the money to start a business is the most difficult thing in the world. Someone may have a good idea, and they'll go to someone who has money and say, "If you'll give me the money and guide me, I'll give you 20% of the business." These people don't understand the real world. Money always gets as much as 80% of the business. It's just a fact of life. Negotiating less percentage is up to you, but know that your percent of something may be better than a higher percent of nothing.

Successful businesses are built a piece at a time. In order to build a business, an entrepreneur must start small, keep spending down and keep reinvesting. Always put the money back into the business. Don't take your rewards until you get your business where you want it to be.

We started our companies small. Our first pizza restaurant franchise started in a 20 square foot, wood-frame building we rented. We had six tables and eight chairs. We mixed the dough by hand, rolled it by hand and baked it in an old baker's oven that wasn't even built to bake at 550∞. It soon burned itself up. We had only one type of pizza, a thin pizza of different varieties and we sold bottled drinks. That was our whole menu. We operated with a very simple philosophy: quality, service and cleanliness.

I was working another job with an insurance company. But, after hours I was in the middle of the pizza operation, along with the other help we hired. I learned to make the pizza, clean the tables and operate the cash register. By doing some of the work myself, I could save the expense of hiring additional employees.

We didn't drain the company of its earnings. We didn't take out earnings and spend them on personal items. Instead, we continued to reinvest. We improved our facility, upgraded our equipment and eventually developed additional stores. Over the last 33 years we have accumulated several hundred restaurants across the United States and even franchised some around the world. We are both franchiser and franchisees. Understanding the psychology of both sides of the franchise community is valuable knowledge. Seeing both viewpoints is especially beneficial in negotiations.

One of our manufacturing companies started the same way. We began with a small building and minimal equipment. Using a philosophy of reinvestment and expense control, we have grown into a national supplier.

We have accomplished our success by maintaining the same conservative approach with which we started. This philosophy has served us well. We continue to use it in the additional companies we have started. If it ain't broke, don't fix it!

One of the pitfalls of understanding and practicing conservatism is that you develop your characteristics and become so ingrained in your nature that when things get successful and it becomes time to enjoy your success, you don't know how. Spending isn't important to you or your conservatism is so much a part of you that you don't really want to be extravagant.

4
Like It or Not, Government Affects Your Business

Government and politics affect business in a number of ways. Volumes have already been written on this topic, so we'll touch on it very briefly. However, this book would not be complete without a mention or overview of one of the primary outside factors that affects business, and that's government.

Decisions by lawmakers at all levels, particularly in regard to taxation, have an effect on business. The more taxes that are levied, the harder it is to accommodate those taxes in business.

Our national politicians and lawmakers are all trying to get a handle on the voting public's attitude toward taxes. Of course, most people are against taxes. However, the increasing number of people requiring and expecting government services means higher taxes. It comes down to a decision of raising taxes and spending to accommodate these needs or lowering taxes and cutting spending and putting some individuals at a hardship to make up the difference. We don't need to get into a debate over taxes and spending cuts, but we do need to talk about the reality of how taxes affect our economy.

Our federal government has made some moves to cut taxes at the federal level. However, they still mandate certain government programs that must be paid for in some manner. These are called "unfunded mandates," and it is increasingly falling on state and local governments to alter their tax structures to take care of these requirements.

Taxation at any level affects business. High taxation at the local level really causes some special problems for a small business. A federal mandate which is not adequately funded falls upon local governments to raise taxes on their citizens.

Take the Americans With Disabilities Act, passed in the early 1990's, which requires all public buildings to become handicapped accessible. Now, this is a compassionate piece of legislation. Most people agree that buildings need to be more accessible to persons with physical disabilities. However, this is also a very costly piece of legislation which has not been adequately funded by the federal government.

In my own community, our city commission found itself faced with having to call a sales tax to pay for renovation and repair of several old facilities, which were not handicapped accessible. The facilities were worn out and needed replacement, but one of the driving forces behind calling the sales tax was to bring these facilities up to the standards mandated by the Americans with Disabilities legislation. The city commission made a good case for passing the sales tax, and the voters approved it by a 3-1 margin.

Then, our county commission had to make a decision on how to fund a new jail mandated by a higher government body. The county commission basically gave the voters a choice of passing a 1/2 cent sales tax or having their property taxes raised for the project. The voters responded by passing the sales tax.

With these two sales tax issues, citizens in my community found their sales taxes raised by one penny for every dollar spent. Now that doesn't sound like much. But, think about the sales tax increase if you are going to buy a car, or an appliance or some other durable good.

My community is located only eight miles from the Missouri state line. Sales and property taxes in Missouri are quite a bit lower than in my community. Here's the rub...businesses in my community who sell cars or appliances or durable goods often have competitors just a short drive away selling the same goods with a lower tax rate.

As this kind of tax structure continues, and there is every indication that it will, communities, counties and states are going to have very different tax bases. In Texas, Nevada and Florida, there is no personal income tax. What does that do to business?

In our increasingly mobile society, we are seeing the effects already. Established, large industries are closing their plants and businesses in the higher taxation areas and relocating them in the lower taxation areas. New businesses and industries are shopping for communities with the lowest tax structure.

Taxes, therefore, have a tremendous effect on where you decide to put your business or where you will expand your business. If you are starting a new business, you need to look very carefully at the current tax structure and try to be intuitive about how that tax base will change over the next few years.

Capital Gains taxes stifle expansion and development of business. Death taxes, (Inheritance and Estate) cause the devastation of some wealth accumulated through the years of hard work and savings (while still paying all the other taxes). In some cases, all the wealth can be lost by forced sale of assets at a lower price than market value just to gain the necessary money to pay death expenses. Whether some taxes are justified or needed, it is wise to remember that <u>all taxes reduce economic activity and increase government spending</u>. That's a fact of life, no matter what your social or political interests may be.

Follow Government Actions

Running a business takes a lot of time. However, government activities can't be ignored by business owners. Business people have to follow what is happening at their level and take actions to impact those decisions made at the local and state level. It is logical and you owe it to yourself to be informed. Talk to your legislators and congressional members. Keep track of the legislation that affects your business and those of your interests, taxes, education, labor and environment issues.

Again, community activism is essential. One of the best ways to impact government decisions is to, in fact, run for elected office. Understandably, that is not for everyone; and realistically, sometimes it is not a good idea for certain businesses or business people to run for office.

If holding public office is not for you, there is another good way to impact government decisions...become active in your local business lobby group, the Chamber of Commerce.

Chambers of Commerce are in business to promote the interest of their members. An active and progressive Chamber is dependent on active progressive Chamber members.

Participate in groups that lobby on behalf of your business or industry. Take an interest in that group's activities. Take action to make sure their representatives reflect your interest and values.

"Lobby" or "Interest Groups" are Not Villains

Lobbyists and "special interest groups" have been resoundingly criticized over the last decade as having too much influence on lawmakers and governmental representatives. Admittedly, some of these lobbying groups have participated in unethical practices, which makes voters wary and suspicious.

However, keep in mind, our government is based on "representation" of our interests and ideas by certain individuals. Since every American can't travel to the state capital or the nation's capital to cast their individual vote on each issue, we cast our vote for an individual we think best represents the interest and ideals we hold dear. Unfortunately, not every person elected is the person we, individually, think best represents us. But, that's the system, and we must all work within its boundaries.

Interest groups are an extension of that representation process. Let's face it, there is strength in numbers. A group of persons acting as a block can have a greater impact on our elected representatives than one single person. Where interest groups step over the line is when they engage in illegal or unethical practices, such as "buying" votes. I'm not advocating this practice at all. In fact, I believe we must hold special interest groups to the same high ethical standards with which we should try to hold ourselves.

We have a responsibility to become an active voice in our government and the issues. Voting is the first tier of action. However, if you are really interested in improving the quality of life for yourself and future generations, you must take it further than that.

Get to know your city council members, your state representative, your state senator, and your congressman. Write or call them about the issues that you feel strongly about. Having served in government positions myself, I know that most people do not take the time to write or call to express their opinion, yet they can be resoundingly critical after the vote is taken. I paid attention to anyone who took the time to personally write or call me about an issue. I may not have agreed with their position, but I appreciated their taking the time and effort to contact me. Any person with the courage to state to their representative their opinion on an issue ranks highly in my mind.

A Visitor From The Past
I had a dream the other night, I didn't understand.
A figure walking through the mist, with flintlock in his hand
His clothes were torn and dirty, as he stood there by my bed.
He took off his three-corned hat, and speaking low, he said,

"We fought a revolution to secure our liberty.
We wrote the Constitution as a shield from tyranny.

For future generations this legacy we gave,
In this land of the free and the home of the brave."

"The freedom we secured for you, we hoped you'd always keep.
But tyrants labored endlessly while your parents were asleep.
Your freedom gone, your courage lost, you're no more than a slave,
In this land of the free and the home of the brave.:

You buy permits to travel, and permits to own a gun.
Permits to start a business, or to build a place for one.
On land that you believe you own, you pay a yearly rent,
Although you have no voice in how the money's spent.

"Your children must attend a school that doesn't educate.
Your Christian values can't be taught according to the state.
You read about your current news, in a regulated press.
You pay a tax you do not owe, to please the I.R.S."

"Your money is no longer made of silver or of gold.
You trade your wealth for paper, so your life can be controlled.
You pay for crime that makes a nation turn from God in shame.
You've take Satan's number, as you've traded in your name."

"You've given government control to those who do you harm,
So they can padlock churches, and steal the family farm.
And keep our country deep in debt, put men of God in jail.
Harass your fellow countrymen, while corrupted courts prevail."

"Your public servants don't uphold the solemn oath they've sworn.
Your daughters visit doctors, so their children won't be born.

Your leadership sends artillery, and guns to foreign shores,
And sends your sons to slaughter, fighting other people's wars."

"Can you regain the freedom for which we fought and died?
Or don't you have the courage, or the faith to stand with pride?
Are there no more values for which you'll fight to save?
Or do you wish your children, to live in fear and be a slave.

"People of the Republic, arise and stand!
Defend the Constitution, the Supreme Law of the land.
Preserve our Great Republic and God given rights.
And pray to God to keep the torch of Freedom burning bright!"

As I awoke he vanished, in the mist from whence he came.
His words were true. We are not free, we have ourselves to blame.
For even now as tyrants trample each God-given right,
We only watch and tremble, too afraid to stand and fight.

If he stood by your bedside, in a dream, while you sleep,
And wonders what remains of your rights he fought to keep,
What would be your answer, if he called out from the grave:
"Is this still the land of the free and home of the brave?"

Government Grinds Slowly For a Reason

As much as we complain that government is "deadlocked" or too slow to respond, it is good advice to remember that there is a reason enacting new laws or legislation takes time. We have a system of government that requires checks and balances all along the way to try to ensure that laws being passed are the best laws possible.

If a law could be passed by one person or one governmental group only, without debate or revisions, we'd have many more laws on the books than we do right now. And, we'd have many more bad laws on the books. True, even with the slow process we have now, some bad laws get through. However, that rate is slowed considerably by the fact that each legislation has to pass through so many checkpoints.

We, as voters and citizens, have the opportunity to reverse laws or legislation we think is detrimental. We can do this by exercising our rights to vote and be an active voice in our government.

The right for people to bring issues to vote through referendums and initiatives is a right that should be passed by legislation. Letting people vote on issues they are concerned about is the purest form of democracy. By petition or privilege it is in the best interest of our citizens to allow government to hear the voice of the people.

Just as term limits should be enacted in our legislative groups, so court (tort) reform should do away with loopholes that impede justice. Victims should have more rights, not less than criminals.

Where is our society headed when it works against free enterprise and the values and rights of its people? Someone said if you took all the wealth and divided it, the same people who currently have the wealth would gradually get it back.

5
Emotion - The New Economic Indicator

When you mention economic indicators, most people think about the Dow average, the unemployment rate, inflation rate, retail sales, etc. as economic indicators, and they'd be right. All these things, plus many more tangible things, like the national debt and interest rates, are all economic indicators.

However, a new and harder-to-grasp economic indicator is emerging very powerfully on the scene, and that economic indicator is emotion. Its impact in today's world is unprecedented. Emotion is playing a tremendous role in the perception of the economic conditions and our behavior or reaction to the economy.

This indicator on buying is controlled by how we "feel" inside. You see it happen over and over again. The pundits give you all the economic indicators that show that the economy should be reacting positively. Yet, sales will slump. Then, they give you negative economic indicators and sales rise. When all the pundits say recession is looming, figures show people are buying more durable goods and spending more money. It's crazy! What is it that is actually driving our economy?

Many times people will buy and sell on the stock market based on their emotional attitudes, not necessarily the economic conditions. This is especially evident in the retail element when you get into finished goods versus putting money into savings or certificates of deposit.

Business people traditionally look to the economic indicators to project how their businesses will perform and what changes need to be made to be more productive. You can't project emotion. You can take all the economic indicators and evaluate them any way you want, but it isn't going to do you any good if the American public decides that this year they are going to buy a new car instead of your appliance. Maybe they decide this is the year they are going to go to the movie theaters rather than stay home and rent videos. It all depends on how the public "perceives" the economy rather than what the economy really is.

So...this is a change. This is where intuition really comes into play. As we look into the future, we must be able to act quickly depending on the American public's emotion.

Guess again! How can you ever determine what reactions you will see in how the public "feels?" Good Luck!

You need to begin an evaluation process. Begin to keep records of what the reaction was to this news or that news. What other factors affected this reaction. Complicated? You bet! You also need to keep track of how we change our review prospects, the Federal Reserves language, the operation of the banking community, Gross National Products...on and on. I think you get the point.

6
The Reality of Investment

Before you invest in anything, do the research and gain the knowledge. Know what you are investing in. Don't take someone else's word for it, especially not the people selling the stuff; they'll lie to you. Remember the story about my "expensive watch."

The idea behind investing is that the product or "thing" you are investing in will grow in value. Speculation and risk are involved in making investments and there are many opportunities to make money...or to go broke.

You can invest in a retail outlet. You can invest in a farm. You can invest in stocks, precious metals, oil, real estate and so on.

There are many ways to invest in real estate. You can buy rental property in which you own the real estate and someone else pays you to use it. You can buy speculative real estate in which you buy a chunk of property, a building or land, and you wait for it to go up in value.

Real Estate is Not an Automatic Money-Maker

Unfortunately for many people who bought into real estate when it was increasing in value, the real estate boom has come to end. The sale of the savings and loans and closing of many banks had a tremendous effect on the value of real estate. It still does today, because not only is it difficult to get a loan, but banks are requiring higher down-payments.

Investing in office buildings used to be much easier than it is today. People used to buy office buildings and rent them out until they depreciated. Because of depreciation, the owner would pay less taxes. When the property ceased depreciating, they would sell it and regain their capital investment (capital gains vs. income tax). Now it's harder to find buyers because loans are harder to get.

If you are looking into real estate to rent, it should have a cash flow that will pay all of your expenses, both fixed and operating costs. You have to look at the percentage of occupancy and make sure that you've got enough of the space rented to cover these costs. In the old days this was easier to do. In many cases, you could get real estate with a low down payment. Often the lenders would only require interest payments for the first two years, allowing the owner time to achieve full occupancy before paying on the principal. Those lenders are hard to find these days.

You can invest in real estate in a number of ways. You can buy land, divide it into lots and sell it off for housing. You can buy land for a shopping center. The key to successful retail investing is finding the marketplace suited for that venture. Obviously, you need to be certain that the land you purchase is zoned for the particular use you want to use it for. Again, do the research.

Farms are probably not a good investment today. As a matter of fact, most of the farms I own I'm trying to sell. Most farmers I talk to tell me how tough it is for farmers right now.

But once again, where there is change there is opportunity. Many entrepreneurs are finding ways to make money through large corporate farming.

Beware of Precious Metals

Investing in precious metals is a concern for me. I'm convinced the precious metals market must make a major revision course in the next few years. It only makes sense because there is no intrinsic value to precious metals. It doesn't support any currency. It doesn't support any monetary systems. What's its value? Only for decorative jewelry! I can't see that those experts who say gold is going to go to $1,000 an ounce really know what they are talking about.

The same situation exists for precious gems. The company that controls the diamond market has rooms packed full of diamonds. They are stored to keep the value up. If they release them all on the market, the value would go down, and then we could all have big diamond rings on our fingers.

If someone wants to give you a gold bar or a diamond, by all means, take it. But, I wouldn't want to invest money in those markets.

7
Opportunities Abound in the International Community

International marketing has provided a new frontier for entrepreneurial pioneers to explore and room to expand business and maximize potential. Along with exciting new opportunities, however, developing foreign enterprise also presents some new challenges and a different set of rules and regulations.

My first encounter outside the continental United States was, as I mentioned earlier, the franchising of a retail food outlet in Vancouver, Canada. Local laws dictated that a percentage of the developing company had to be owned by citizens of that country. This law is quite common, one which we have run into in other countries as well. This requirement of domestic ownership challenged us to find a local partner that we had not known prior to the development. Of course, it is extremely important to know your associates. To make up for this lack of knowledge, we had to be very careful with our contract, writing a specific and complete set of guidelines for the partnership. By listing and covering all possible contingencies, we tried to avoid any further disagreements, or even worse, litigation. It is very difficult to make partnerships work. I have often said they don't work at all. Now, we were in a situation where we had to make the best of a partnership in which we didn't even know the partner beforehand.

We were challenged again on this project when we began to look for suppliers of our ingredients. Since this was a franchise, there were very strict requirements on quality, design, service and trademarks. Everything was to be standardized and duplicated according to the franchise requirement. However, because of health department restrictions and embargoes that prevented international shipping of many food products, it was impossible to have our ingredients shipped from the U.S.. So, naturally, we had to purchase them locally.

Variations between the ingredients available in the U.S. and those available in Canada and the franchise restrictions complicated matters even further. The butterfat contents of an ingredient, for example, had to be changed to comply with the new Canadian codes. Many compromises had to be made and too many compromises could significantly alter the quality of the product. We had to keep the final product as close as possible to the original and acceptable to the customer. Even though we were only a few hundred miles away from the U.S., we may as well have been thousands.

In this particular venture, there were not any major problems with real estate, locations, equipment and marketing. The language was the same, and there is cooperation between Canada and the United States. Our international venture worked out quite nicely and was well worth the effort. In many other countries, these aspects could present many problems.

International Business Presents Challenges

In international business, research and planning become especially important. You will often be dealing with cultures, economies, governments and geographies very different from our own. Plan your business, just as you must plan domestic business, but don't assume anything about the situation will be the same. Research carefully. Don't let ignorance of these differences ruin a great opportunity.

Cultural Considerations

Cultural differences can present may challenges. Different religious practices, cultural taboos, customs and prejudices may affect the acceptability of your product or service. If you plan to produce a food product in a foreign country, for example, certain ethnic beliefs or customs of that country may require you to add or remove some ingredients from your product to make it acceptable to the culture.

Relations with the labor force of foreign countries can offer many new challenges to U.S. companies who choose to produce and/or market internationally. Work ethics and attitudes toward companies vary significantly around the globe. Some work forces in Japan, for example, have a lifetime commitment to their company, and in return, expect to be taken care of by the company. In other countries, however, the workers may feel no alliance whatsoever to their employers.

Research the particular labor system in the country. They may be drastically different from our own. In some countries, factories alternate between crews. One crew will work for a week or a month, and then get a week or a month off while the second crew works. The work ethics are different. In some places, after getting some money, the workers don't want to work for awhile.

Religious obligations may also impact the labor system. If workers must attend prayer several times a day, the work schedule must be altered to accommodate them.

Distribution and delivery of product, utility availability, refrigeration...all the things that seem simple in this country could be a problem elsewhere.

The work force's response to authority can be another significant variable. Some cultures are very obedient to authority, while others rebel against it. Different attitudes provide different productivity levels, require different methods for training and retraining and significantly affect the way a U.S. company will do business in a foreign country.

Economic Considerations

In foreign markets, you must research your customer base. Find out what they can afford to pay for your product or service. Then determine what price you must place on your product or service to make a profit. Obviously, if they cannot afford the necessary price, then, regardless of the demand for the product, you cannot proceed with the venture.

The availability and cost of real estate is another important consideration. The cost or rental price of property may make profits impossible. You need to be aware of these considerations before entering into international markets.

The availability and cost of marketing and advertising is another key concern. Opportunities to advertise in the media may not be available in many countries, or the costs may make advertising impossible.

You may have to decide whether to export your product from the U.S. or to produce it in a foreign country. Your decision will be based on the selling price, cost of shipping and local production costs.

Trading For Profit

The currency in some countries is so volatile that its value fluctuates dramatically from day to day. In such a market, without daily exchange, there is an enormous risk to cost and profit. Therefore, to operate in some markets you must learn to trade for profit.

In Brazil and now Mexico, inflation rates are double digit and spiraling. The value of their currency isn't stable enough to trade on the international market. If you have a currency everyone wants, like the dollar, it is easy to trade anywhere. But if you are trading for pesos, by the time you get around to using them, they may not be worth nearly as much as you paid for them. So, rather than dealing with the peso, most international traders would want to exchange for value-added products, material goods which can then be traded for valuable currency.

When Pepsi-Cola went into Russia to sell their soft drinks, they couldn't take the ruble. It wasn't a tradable currency. So they exchanged Pepsi-Cola syrup for vodka. Other countries have traded with Siberia for pelts.

Different situations may require different means of trading for profit. If you have a retail outlet in China, for instance, you would be receiving Chinese currency from your customers. But, the Chinese currency is not tradable on the international market. You may decide to trade your currency within China for silk or leather goods. You may, in fact, have to trade two or three times before you have a valuable product to trade for currency outside China. In any situation, however, getting value back for the value given is the priority.

It is very important, when dealing in foreign markets, to work with bankers and accountants that specialize in foreign trade. Perform background checks, research sales analysis and surveys to make sure you can ultimately end up with the currency and profit you want.

Government Considerations

Research all laws that pertain to business. Many countries have unique restrictions and regulations. Some restrict private ownership of property. Some have a nationalization rule that allows the government to take over businesses. Many oil companies have lost wells to governments through nationalization. Find and use an attorney who specializes in international business.

Geographical Considerations

Consider all aspects of geography. Natural resources may be limited in an area. Transportation may be a problem. If you ship a product to a country and they don't have the means of getting it to the consumer, you will obviously have problems. You can't provide products that require refrigeration to areas that don't have electricity. You can't put equipment in an area that won't have the people to maintain and repair it. You must consider the climate. How would a monsoon season affect your business? You must investigate every aspect of the area in which you intend to do business. Obstacles can arise where you would least expect them.

Adapt and be Flexible

Creativity and ingenuity are necessary for doing business anywhere, but they are especially needed in international business. The development and expansion of your marketplace, sales, and profits are not always going to be black and white; you must learn to work in the gray areas. If you aren't willing to find the way to do business, you will be too easily discouraged and will not climb the mountain but stumble over the mole hill.

You must be prepared to adapt your concept to the foreign location. Our restaurant interiors are adapted to the local preference and availability of materials. A striking example of this is our 300+ seat restaurant in Hong Kong, which features the very bright and open ambiance popular in Asian countries.

Intuition becomes especially important in international business. You must be aware, at all times, of the possibility of change. In many countries, the government can change overnight, or neighborhoods can be overtaken by warring factions. Uncertainty is the rule in these locations. Plan to pay for your business or location as quickly as possible so that if conditions change, at least you've recovered your investment. It doesn't hurt so badly to close something down if you've already paid for it.

The International Business Climate

The economic outlook in the U.S. can be improved through international marketing. U. S. companies that market in foreign lands will have increased sales. With increases in sales, the companies will pay more taxes. Ultimately, increased taxes will help decrease our national debt.

Over the last 50 years, many U. S. companies, especially automobile and technology industries, have lost a large share of their market to foreign competitors. As a result, the U.S. has had a significant trade deficit which has had a negative impact on our economy. If more U.S. companies would take advantage of new opportunities on the international scene, the balance of trade could be turned around, strengthening the U. S. economy.

There is no longer a basis of value or true support base for any currency in the world, including the United States. The gold and silver-backed currency from the days of our forefathers is forever a myth. We don't have enough gold to support a very large percentage of our outstanding currency. This means that technically all countries are broke. There are strengths of economy and gross national production to go along with taxation income to support the confidence of currency more so in some communities than others, but we are still supporting economies through a credit format, natural resources, productivity of products and goods and gross national production.

Many countries, which in the past have attempted to maintain an independence from global economics, are beginning to realize that their own economies depend upon international business. They are beginning to make it easier for international companies to do business in their countries.

While on a trip to the Far East to survey business opportunities, I met a representative from a Minneapolis company that had a plant in the Philippines and had just opened another in Thailand. He was quick to point out that Thailand's import and export restrictions made it more difficult to do business in Thailand than in the Philippines. This was mentioned to the military and government leaders of Thailand, and we believe that through their efforts the country is making attempts to improve their laws pertaining to free enterprise. This is observed by Stanton J. Paris in <u>A Question of Currency</u>. I think this same kind of thing must and will occur throughout the world.

You never know where opportunity will be found. You need to learn where the obstacles will be. Doing international business can be difficult and involved. The opportunities are great and plentiful if you have the right product and a workable price. Meet the challenge head on with determination and a desire for fun, and you will be rewarded with positive results.

8
The Economic and Global Picture in Today's Marketplace
and
Forecasting for Conditions into the Next Century

Good management strategy is understanding economics and trends. Our economic conditions change rapidly, and it is important to be intuitive about what those conditions might be two, five and ten years from now.

As we move into the 21st century, we are in what might be called a cynical trend. Most individuals believe we face a very gloomy future unless we resolve several economic topics, foremost the balanced budget. As we look at the cycle of our government and the cycle of the business community, we will find that trends seem to follow and repeat themselves, such as recessions, inflationary periods and the rise and fall of the stock market.

Many people believe that if you follow the graphic trends of those changes as they have occurred, when they have gone through the peaks and valleys, you will find similarities responsive enough to help make better business decisions based on the time frame that you are approaching, and the characteristics that have expended themselves in the past.

Lending Crisis of the 1980's has Made Entrepreneurship Harder to Obtain

Entrepreneurship has become less and less easy to obtain, primarily because of the domestic focus and lending practices based on the 1980's savings and loan crisis and the dilemma that it has stemmed within our economic system. Those losses essentially have had to be recouped through taxes and government repayment of those losses.

The savings and loan crisis occurred primarily because of the high profits taken and loans too easily arranged with little equity base. Contractors on residential and commercial buildings would inflate the cost of construction and achieve large profits from construction. In turn, those individuals buying the inflated properties were able to do so with little equity base, small down payments and relatively high interest rates based on current market conditions. As long as the economy and the rental base afforded it, they would continue to exist and hold on to the ownership of those properties. Once conditions began to slack, through loss of employment or inflation or for whatever reason, it was too easy to quit making rental payments and let the properties go back to the lending institutions. Suddenly, lending institutions found themselves holding many properties. Because of federal regulations, they were forced to sell those properties at auction or fire sales and could not recover the amount of the loan through the selling price. The situation brought about the failure of many of those institutions.

The same type of crisis appeared in the banking industry, both in the urban and rural markets. Some bankers were making inflated loans based on their own methods of appraisal and based on the current market and economic conditions. A prime example of this is in farm loans where the price of farm acreage inflated itself over a 20-year period of time and established land values far exceeding the economic returns on the crops they would grow or livestock they would raise. As a result of these loans, many banks had to close their doors because they were not able to cover the amount of reserves and capital that were required by federal and state laws.

These dilemmas have made it much more difficult for entrepreneurs of the 1990's and into the 21st century to start new businesses and developments. Loans have become much more difficult to obtain. Loans are made only to those who have net worth and reserves to back them up. Therefore, the individual without access to large capital amounts or enough financial worth to provide security for loans are finding it harder to go into business for themselves.

The increased pressure on lending institutions to provide more security and collateral will continue to force them to limit the number of individuals who will qualify for loans under their standards. You can expect additional interest and fee charges through the lending institutions as they try to improve their profit and loss statements and, also, recoup some of the losses they have incurred in the past and losses they will incur in the future.

I believe this situation has had an effect on the increased division in our social structure in reference to upper class, middle class and lower class. The trend into the 21st century will be an increasingly shrinking middle class, an increase in lower class and little change in upper class. This will happen in corporate levels as well. The big corporations will get bigger and the smaller corporations will get smaller or become non-existent.

More Monopolies are Being Created

The continued increase and size of the large corporations and the diminishing existence of smaller corporations means a different type of capital structure. This is influenced by those companies who have close semblance to monopolies and who control the cost of those goods by creating less competition. This will influence the way we enter into the 21st century. The positioning of large corporate giants will affect the type of accounting, the type of sales price evaluation and market conditions. You will see within the government, attempts to operate on a basis similar to the corporate world. You will see a deeper instinct as to providing profit centers within the government operations and a much more sophisticated approach to getting the best price on goods and product purchases. Also, better control of contractors in aerospace, military construction and vehicles and all of the other products relative to government purchasing. Currently many appointed buyers for the government receive a percentage of the purchase price as their salary or part of it. Naturally this prompts the agent to seek the highest price available.

Balancing the Budget is Essential

In just a few years, the U. S. has gone from being the Number One lender in the world to being the Number One debtor. Much of this is because our real gross national product has diminished and has not taken a leading position as exports have fallen below imports. The American public and federal lawmakers have finally realized this crisis. The need for balancing the budget, the attention to being more competitive in the world marketplace and decreasing the federal deficit are now priorities. Unless we address this crisis, we surely will not maintain world stature as the leading economic nation. The challenge is to find the competitive edge to produce products that will be sold on an international basis, to regain our position in automobile sales, aircraft sales, electronics and farm equipment and all of the items pertinent to strong international sales.

Much is discussed about the fact that American citizens have caused our nation to be a spending society rather than a saving society. The savings ratio in the U.S. compared to Japan is dismal. The Japanese are very conservative and thrifty in setting aside a good portion of their earnings in savings for future use. In America, we have become a spending society whereas credit cards and other types of credit purchases have led people to buy now and pay later. This continues to be the demise of our economic condition, primarily because a lot of the debt and lending is coming from overseas institutions to take those earnings back as a boost to their own economies. The challenge in this country is to try to encourage more domestic savings and be more competitive in the production of goods and materials.

Referring back to personal spending habits and the lack of saving in this country, we find that the tendency to spend declines in certain business expansion periods and in retrospect, saving rises when there is some concern about the economic future. It is interesting to note how recession can be viewed by every economist in a different way and the time frames allotted to those recessionary or inflationary periods be so variable from different individuals based on the factors they use for informational input.

The political aspects of economic policy are always something of an exonerating nature. It is interesting to look at government operations relative to the public's opinion about how our country is doing economically. The public holds the President accountable for the economy, rather than the Congress, which is where it really belongs. In this way, the fiscal policy of government is perceived in an entirely different way than the fiscal policy of private enterprise. As citizens we will never get efficient government, lower taxes or control of our deficits until we find a way to monitor and control spending. We must become more cost conscious and protect our funds and tax money from government officials and politicians who are spending money that isn't theirs. Until we are able to do this, balanced budgets and national debts will continue to be a problem.

I have found that unless you have something to lose it isn't necessary to worry about what you are spending or what it costs. Human nature and human behavior patterns are not to worry about being conservative. But if we are to persevere as an economic world leader we must become more conservative.

The Prognosis for Business in the Late 1990's and Early 21st Century

Today's conditions have prompted the acquisition market in the banking community. What we are seeing is the absorption of small and mid-size banks by the giants of banking. The large banks are buying the small ones and thereby limiting the options in banking.

The costs, fees and charges by banks for their services and therefore the cost of banking and borrowing will escalate into exorbitant prices to consumers and huge profits for the banks. The banking community has gone from depressed profits to a very healthy earnings profit. Personal and business banking will never be inexpensive again unless we develop more competition.

Changing of the Business Climate

The business climate has changed dramatically over the last century. I can remember as a small boy that the downtown area, especially in the small towns, was the highlight of Saturday night. That's when all the shopping was done. That's where people gathered on Friday and Saturday nights to shop and just mingle through the streets of town. Maybe they would stop and get something to eat, pick up some popcorn, visit the soda fountains for an ice cream or malt, or just stand on the corner and visit with friends. The streets were bustling with people walking up and down. The businesses were all small family owned places. One business would trade with another. The jeweler would trade with the clothing store. The clothing store would trade with the insurance agency. The insurance agency would trade with the hardware store. The hardware store would trade with the drugstore, the drugstore with the dentist, the dentist with the doctor, the doctor with the restaurants, and it went on and on. The money in the community would circulate about 13 times.

Today's climate is very different. Big business has developed huge discount stores, huge department stores, huge grocery store and food marts. Restaurants have become very sophisticated in size and specialization. The whole business climate has changed. The super stores still have their weaknesses. They can't provide as much service. They can't offer some of the assistance that an individual can offer, so the small business still has an opportunity to come back.

The business climate will continue to change and change again. Home shopping is becoming very prominent. This will cause yet another change in the way we shop and what we buy. Carry-out food is becoming very popular. Rather than eating out at a restaurant, many families are choosing to purchase prepared food and then returning home to eat. It is a transition daily. It is not any specific format that is going to become consistent. As we see the business climate change, we have people specializing in specific areas like office supplies. Even as we see the big discount stores who carry everything developing, we also see specialty stores that specialize in just one segment, just one type of appliance, or appliances in general flourishing. We have food courts in most major malls, where there are multiple kinds of food, all served in the same general area. At the other end of that spectrum we have coffee shops and bagel shops that are cropping up everywhere and thriving.

It is interesting and curious to watch as new ideas spring forth. The entrepreneurial spirit is developing a system or an idea or a business that people will accept as the way they want their merchandise.

For more information about this book and other
publications by:

Williams Publishing
Books that Inform, Educate and Inspire

We welcome your responses and suggestions. If you would like to
share your thoughts or feelings after reading this book, please write
or call and tell us about your experience. We especially would like to
hear about any positive changes or rewarding experiences in your life
related to this book.

Gene Bicknell has also recorded two wonderful CDs of songs, both
available on Ringtail Records. We know that you will love them!

* *Old Glory* * and * *Viagra Man* *

by Gene Bicknell

To order:

Call (620) 231-3390 ext. 106

Credit Cards Accepted

To contact the author regarding his schedule for upcoming work-
shops and seminars or to be placed on our mailing list for our other
outstanding publications please contact:

Williams Publishing
203 E. Laverne Way

Palm Springs, California 92264

Telephone: (760) 318-3407

Fax: (760) 327-7651 E-mail: PSBill@aol.com

To contact Mr. Bicknell call: (620) 231-3390 ext. 106